THE Wit
— AND —
Wisdom
OF
OZZY
OSBOURNE

✝

DAVE THOMPSON

Published by

Krause Publications, a division of F+W Media, Inc.
700 East State Street • Iola, WI 54990-0001
715-445-2214 • 888-457-2873
www.krausebooks.com

To order books or other products call toll-free 1-800-258-0929
or visit us online at www.krausebooks.com or www.Shop.Collect.com

Cover image: Getty Images/Myrna Suarez

Library of Congress Control Number: 2010923992

ISBN-13: 978-1-4402-1400-4
ISBN-10: 1-4402-1400-X

Cover Design by Claudean Wheeler
Designed by Shawn Williams
Edited by Kristine Manty

Printed in the United States

Contents

Introduction

"Bubbles! Oh come on Sharon! I'm fucking Ozzy Osbourne, I'm the Prince of fucking Darkness. Evil! Evil! What's fucking evil about a shitload of bubbles!"

Search for Ozzy Osbourne on the Internet, and chances are that remark will be one of the first hits you get. Because, more than all the millions and millions of words that have been written *about* him, those fractured sentences uttered *by* him best sum up the sheer dichotomy of the man.

To many people, those who have followed his career since 1970, or have picked up on his music in the four decades since then, Ozzy *is* the Prince of Darkness, a man whose music has soundtracked so many demonic fantasies that, if it's true what they say about the Devil having all the best songs, then Ozzy's been stuffing his jukebox for forty years.

To those who discovered him through *The Osbournes* reality show, though, he's a family man as well, one who may act crazy when the cameras are on, but who really likes nothing better than to settle down with his family, watch TV, and then relax in… a bubble bath? Well, maybe not.

This book is about both of those personas, and a handful more besides. It depicts Ozzy from every angle: the family man and the Prince of Darkness, the politician and the sex object, the drunkard, the druggie, and the epitome of sobriety. It is about rock 'n' roll and how it can save your soul, and modern life and how it damns it. There will be moments of laugh-out-loud comedy, and scratch-your-head craziness. He will deliver some shocking confessions, then turn around and confess that he's shocked. There will be moments of deep introspection, and tenderness, too.

But most of all, there will be Ozzy, pure and unadulterated, four decades worth of his ripest ripostes, oddest observations, deepest dreams, and most articulate answers. Yeah, articulate. Because he might come over like a crazy person when you watch him on TV or hear him on the radio, but when you sit down and seriously consider what he's saying…

Well, he said it best. He's fucking Ozzy Osbourne. And he's got a few things to tell you.

But first…

First, I'd like to tell you a story.

Riffing on the name of one of Britain's best-loved candies, Ozzy Osbourne shrugged disdainfully in the early 1980s: "The nearest Sabbath ever came to Black Magic was a box of chocolates."

At the end of 1968, however, it was difficult for anybody, confirmed chocoholic or otherwise, to avoid some reflection on the Dark Arts. Scything out of the psychedelic underground as it searched desperately for fresh alternatives to the rules of the establishment, the successor (logical or otherwise) to the Beatles' drive into transcendental meditation, Satanism was the counter-culture's next big thrill and, from the Sunday tabloids to the Rolling Stones—opposite poles that had hitherto rarely agreed on anything—it lay correspondingly upon everybody's lips.

"We have become very interested in magic," Stone Keith Richard warned the *Sunday Express*. "We are very serious about this."

And there was more. Study the faces arrayed on the Beatles' *Sgt Pepper's Lonely Hearts Club Band* sleeve, and influential English occultist Aleister Crowley peers out from there as well. British blues legend Graham Bond, whose Organization band proved the seminal training ground for some of the later 1960s' greatest instrumentalists (Cream's Jack Bruce among them), was a loudly practicing occultist; and Jimmy Page, at that time guitarist with the Yardbirds (but later to fly Led Zeppelin to glory), had friends all over the world seeking out diabolic literature for his personal library. It was already common knowledge that the Devil had all the best music. Now it seemed as though he had all the best musicians as well.

It was guitarist Tony Iommi who first voiced aloud the thought that his band, Earth, could do a lot worse than attach their own star to the underworld firmament.

Iommi, vocalist Ozzy Osbourne, bassist Geezer Butler, and drummer Bill Ward had already been playing together for a couple of years, during which time Earth had developed a great reputation around their native city of Birmingham, England. But that was all they had, a reputation—and the dubious honor of Iommi having spent four days as a member of Jethro Tull at the end of 1968.

What they needed now was something to transform that reputation into reality; something that would make people sit up and pay attention. Glancing out at the cinema that stood across the road from the band's garage rehearsal space, watching the queues of customers patiently awaiting whatever was showing that week, the quartet mused aloud about how it was always the horror films that drew the longest lines. It was the age of the Hammer Studios' greatest epics, the seemingly endless litany of variations on Bram Stoker's *Dracula;* but, equally, it was an age that had been irrevocably flavored by the success of Roman Polanski's *Rosemary's Baby*, a genuinely frightening film that didn't simply tap into the prevalent counter-culture zeitgeist; it stormed it in a manner that the likes of the Rolling Stones could only dream of.

Neither was it the cinema alone that was making money hand-over-cloven hoof, nor merely the music industry that was so delightedly dancing with the devil. For every unreformed hippy kid who still sat in a park, his nose buried in *The Hobbit* or the *I-Ching*, there were now three times as many fearlessly devouring the works of Dennis Wheatley, the greatest of all Britain's pulp occult authors. From the war pigs snuffling in the trough of Vietnam, to the hollow hell of starvation and famine in Biafra, civilization itself was bracing for an encounter with the Dark Lord, and Osbourne couldn't help but wonder: if people were willing to pay good money to be scared by a movie or a book, how much would they pay to be scared by a rock band?

Earth had already driven their sound into a dark, almost stygian, cavern, a bludgeoning of enormous riffs, a tsunami of bass and percussion and, over it all, a vocal that shrieked and whooped like a banshee. It was a primeval sound, one that seemed to predate even the most barbarous rock 'n' roll in its unerring reduction of its component elements to one solid wall of slow-moving, gut-shaking, heart-haunting noise.

But the further Earth moved away from the standard blues and rock 'n' roll covers that were their regular repertoire, the further their chances of finding an audience seemed to recede. If they were to succeed, they needed to begin again—same sound, same musicians, but a very different name and a very different image.

Osbourne's horror rock idea was a sound one, to be sure. But, according to Ward, it was still a major decision.

In the end, the decision was made for them, the evening on which Earth were booked to play the prestigious Birmingham Ballroom. They'd sensed something was amiss the moment they arrived at the venue, and saw the best-dressed audience of their lives, older than the usual Earth crowd...older, in fact, than any band's crowd.

The audience, too, shifted uneasily as it watched four unkempt, hairy musicians make their way across the stage, to pick up and plug in their electric guitars. Unbeknownst to Osbourne, Ward, Iommi, and Butler, another band named Earth had recently emerged on the local scene, one that not only had money and influence behind it, but also the respectability conferred by their note-perfect recreations of an old-time orchestral dance band. The promoter had booked the wrong Earth.

Earth played a handful of driving blues numbers to an almost preternatural silence, then fled the stage. Now, back in the garage, they knew that it was time to make the long-simmering name change.

Earth played their final show under that name at the London Marquee on March 11, 1969; with near-optimum timing (and, of course, not a little forethought) they would make their debut as Black Sabbath at the same venue two nights later, on March 13. The only thing that spoiled the symbolism was the calendar itself—the date fell on a Thursday that year.

The original *Black Sabbath* is a 1963 horror film directed by Italian Mario Bava and starring Boris Karloff as both a vampire and as the linkman between the three tales that comprise the movie. Known in the USA as *The Three Faces of Fear*, *Black Sabbath* had proven an enduringly successful film in the UK. It also happened to be one of the four members of Earth's all-time favorite films—and a damned good band name as well.

It certainly seemed to be well omened. As the band rehearsed together the same evening that they adopted the new name, Butler and Iommi were both messing around with some riffs they'd come up with, seeing if anything gelled—when suddenly it did, their independent noodlings slamming together as though they'd been playing the song all their lives.

It was a magical moment, and it only got better. Ward picked up his drum sticks and began, tentatively at first, but with increasing confidence, to play along. Then

Ozzy took the microphone and started to sing the first words that came into his head…"What is this that stands before me?"

The song that would become both the group's anthem and its statement of intent was born and, though its eventual title would never make its way into the lyric, even before they'd finished playing, Ozzy knew what he wanted to call the song. Like the band itself, it was to be "Black Sabbath."

Relaunching themselves onto the local circuit, reintroducing themselves to Earth's old hangout at Henry's Blueshouse, Black Sabbath quickly found that news of their name was traveling fast. Overnight, audiences that once comprised shiftless blues

Bill Ward, Ozzy, Geezer Butler, and Tony Iommi at the start of their careers.

fans and hapless passers-by, seemed to be solidifying into something else entirely, a gathering of pale young men and deathly white women who, clad in black and festooned in silver, literally haunted the edges of Henry's Blueshouse, scarcely moving, barely applauding, but driving the band on through the force of their will alone.

This energy affected the band. The lyrics got darker, the bass got louder, they stopped wearing jeans and started turning up in all-black, with little silver pentagrams and symbols. And that's when the rumors started to fly—rumors that were ripped straight out of the day's tabloid headlines.

Geezer Butler has long believed that Black Sabbath had a spirit that looked out for them, a "fifth member" of the group that none of the others could see or speak with, but which was always by their side—at least until the rival deities of chemicals, alcohol, money, and ego conspired to chase it away. His name was Henry, Butler said, smiling—but it was a smile that acknowledged merely the mundanity of the name when applied to so miraculous a presence. Henry himself was no laughing matter.

Most of the time, Henry simply concerned himself with the business of the band, a helping hand at rehearsal, a guiding thought in songwriting, a beacon of inspiration that, ultimately, led Black Sabbath not simply to fame and fortune, but to levels of success that exceeded even their bravest dreams. Right now, though, Henry maybe had something else to concern himself with, although it would be another couple of months before Black Sabbath discovered precisely what that was.

They were playing a club in the north of England, nobody remembers precisely where, when a self-described witch told them that a slighted coven had indeed placed a curse on them, consigning them to a life of shattered dreams and broken spirits.

Ozzy said nothing, but the visitor watched him thoughtfully finger the crucifix that his father had made for him. Then she shook her head and answered the question that he hadn't even thought of asking yet. "No, those things didn't have anything to do with it. They do look good, though. You should keep them on."

PHOTO CREDITS

The images in this book are copyright to the following:

P. 4: AP photo/Hard Rock Cafe, Diane Bondareff
P. 9: Warner Bros. Records/Rhino Media
P. 12: Epic Records
P. 21: AP photo/Douglas Pizac
P. 28: Warner Bros. Records/Rhino Media
P. 39: AP photo/Rusty Kennedy
P. 42: Fin Costello photo/Jet Records
P. 51: Fin Costello photo/Jet Records
P. 56: AP file photo
P. 63: AP photo/Electronic Arts
P. 68: Joseph Cultice photo/Sony Music
P. 74: Sony Music Entertainment
P. 83: AP photo
P. 94: Jet Records
P. 105: Mark "Weissguy" Weiss photo/CBS Associated
P. 113: AP photo/Lacy Atkins
P. 118: Joseph Cultice photo/Sony Music
P. 122: AP photo
P. 127: AP photo/Evan Agostini
P. 133: AP Photo/Jeff Geissler
P. 138: AP photo/FOX, Joseph Cultice
P. 143: De Laurentiis Entertainment Group/Lorimar Home Video
P. 148: AP photo/Damian Dovarganes
P. 155: Gene Kirkland photo/Epic
P. 162: Gene Kirkland photo/Epic
P. 169: AP photo/Evan Agostini
P. 170: AP photo/Matt Sayles

CHAPTER 1

GROWING UP OZZY

ohn Michael Osbourne was born on December 3, 1948, in Aston, a suburb of the English midlands city of Birmingham. The city, like the country, was still recovering from six years of World War Two—Birmingham, one of Britain's major industrial hubs, had been damaged heavily by German bombing and many businesses were still struggling to pull themselves out of the bombsites and craters that littered the metropolis.

His parents were lucky enough to have jobs with two of the companies that were back on their feet. Ozzy's father, John senior, was a toolmaker at GEC, while his mother, Lillian, worked for Lucas, a company that made auto components. With five children to support, they needed all the income they could raise.

Today, an army of sociologists and psychologists would very likely flock to describe his childhood and upbringing as "under-privileged" but at the time, it was normal. Almost without exception, the generation of British rock musicians that rose up during the mid- to late 1960s (and beyond) were raised under similar circumstances, by parents who fought to put food on the table, amid the rubble and debris of the most destructive war the world, let alone a tiny island off the coast of Europe, had ever seen.

Labor relations were poor, as companies struggled to save every penny they could, often at the expense of their workforce's paycheck, and the only future that was mapped out for the children being born in those years was the same gray, monotonous routine that had already consumed their parents, their grandparents, and so on back in time. You left school at fifteen and found a job in a factory. At eighteen, you would be called up for National Service—eighteen months of compulsory service in the military. You would then be released back into the workforce, to hope that your old job was still available. And there you would remain until you retired at sixty-five. Then you died.

Of course there were escape routes. A gifted athlete or sportsman might carve out a few years of glory in his late teens and twenties, a talented thespian might break into theater, film, or even the new-fangled television (assuming it wasn't just another technological gimmick that would blink out of sight the moment something better came along). A good musician might land on his or her feet in one of the many dance bands and orchestras that then toured the ballrooms and nightclubs of the land.

But every one of those options demanded one thing. Talent…and a prodigious talent at that. There was no democracy in the arts or sports worlds back then; no grassroots circuit on which a merely "able" performer might be able to muddle by. Either you had "it" or you didn't, and the young Ozzy Osbourne probably didn't know what "it" even was.

Then rock 'n' roll came along, and the rules changed overnight. Suddenly there was an alternative, and with it, ambition and aspiration. For the first time, a generation didn't have to content itself with merely dreaming about a glorious future. For the first time, kids could look about and see that future unfolding all around.

Even kids like Ozzy.

"When I was born, I weighed
ten pounds something like fourteen
ounces. I was one of the biggest children
ever — they thought I was twins, you know?
The midwife said to my mother, 'This guy
is going to be huge.' I swear to God,
it's the God's honest truth.
Destiny rules me, man."

(1982)

"My mother was an amateur singer,
my father was an amateur drunk."

"If I could change anything about myself,
I'd give myself the serenity I've been
looking for since I was a kid."

"I tried to strangle my younger
brother 'cause I hated him."

(1982)

"I come from a rather large family, three older sisters and two younger brothers. I've had a very, very unique life. I often sit back and remember when I had no money—when you're in the middle of it, you get depressed, thinking it's going to last forever. All of a sudden, out of nowhere—a bolt of lightning—here I am!"

(Launch.com, 10/30/1998)

"I'm very well off; I've got property all over the place, I've had a very fruitful career. But I've never had a number one album in America. But I've lasted several generations and somebody says to me, 'Do you notice any difference in the audience?' I've been doing it now for thirty years. Some of the fans are older, but I've picked up new fans along the way."

(Launch.com, 10/30/1998)

"My father hated his brother Harold—my whole family's fucking nuts; my sister's been committed twice. For real—she's like fucking over the top. My other sister's an absolute neurotic wreck. My whole family has this fucking thing of lunacy, you know? I use my lunacy for better ends."

(1982)

"My neurotic sister Iris...once she'd cleaned the house, you couldn't move. You couldn't breathe, you couldn't touch a thing, you couldn't eat. You had to sit there. And I got up and beat the shit out of her. Blacked both her eyes, and fucking pounded her around the room. I thought I'd better go and see my father...'cause he's going to kill me when he comes back and sees the sight of her face. Sure enough the bus comes, fucking off the bus, he's singing his fucking lungs off on the bus and getting the bus revved up. I said, 'Daddy, I've just beaten Iris up.' He says, 'Good job. Fucking 'bout time you fucking whacked her'.**"**

"I left school at fifteen, went to work, and cut my thumb off the first fucking day. Sewed it back on.**"**

(1982)

"My father was a fucking gem. I got my front from my father, and my singing voice from my mother.**"**

"I was the classiest fucking shoplifter
you ever met in your life. Coat over the
arm, 'Scuse me, sir'—bong! Gone.
I'm a rock and roll rebel."

(1982)

"I was the kind of nutter people
liked to be around—I'd do anything.
Basically I was the clown, I always have been.
I was never a bad guy. When I got successful, it
gave me a ticket to be a lunatic, but I didn't do
it with any malice, apart from whacking the
wife 'round the ear now and again."

(Independent, 2009)

"I was always dirty and smelly. The kids
teased me unmercifully, which is why I spent
the first bit of money I earned from music
on drugs and strong fucking cologne."

"I tried to hang myself once.
I thought I wanted to find out what it's
like to be hung. In England, you get these
fucking terraced houses, and you get things they
call entries, sort of alleyways, and you get these
bars on the entries. I thought, well, I want to
hang myself—this is God's honest truth. So I got
my mother's washing line, made a noose, put it
over the bar in the entry, then fucking jumped
off the chair and held the rope. I thought, 'If I'm
gonna die, I'll let go of the rope and I'll fucking be
okay.' My father come out of the house and caught
me doing it, and he beat the shit out of me.
I thought, 'Fuck, I should have
done it for real.'"

(1982)

"I suffered from dyslexia and attention deficit disorder. Nobody knew what it was—they used to sit you in the corner with a dunce's hat."

(Independent, 2009)

"I set fire to my sister once. Didn't like her. I poured gasoline on her skirt and set fire to her. I got beaten round the fuckin' house, as usual."

(1982)

"When you're young, you're stupid. You do silly things. I did (the O-Z-Z-Y tattoo across his knuckles) when I was 14. I could have had it removed, but why? It's my trademark. People stop me and say, 'Let me have a look at your hand.'"

(Launch.com 10/30/1998)

"I used to wear, you know these kitchen sets, these cleavers? Butchers' cleavers? Where I came from, it was kill or be killed."

Ozzy was sitting pretty in 1981 and enjoying the commercial success of his first solo album, *Blizzard of Ozz*, certified four times platinum in the U.S. (a feat he again achieved with 1991's *No More Tears*). *Blizzard Of Ozz* is one of very few albums to achieve such certification without the benefit of a Top 40 single.

"I was in for burglary. I used to work
with this Irish guy called Pascal Donegal.
He used to go and clock houses, find out when
people went to work, then we'd burgle them.
This time the idiot didn't realize the house he was
watching was a boarding house. People had gone
to work but the owner was on night shift and
he was still in bed. When we broke in he
beat seven shades of shit out of us.**"**

(Sounds, 1981)

"I was good at playing truant.**"**

(Mojo)

"I got three months—it was burglary,
larceny, assault, ABH, and possessing dope all in
one thing. Mind you, I was on the run at the time
so I quite liked the nick—free food, free tobacco.
It was heaven to me, 'cos I'd had no dough.
I shared a cell with a murderer. He used to tell
me about all the ways he'd killed people.
I quite got into it at the time.**"**

(Sounds, 1981)

"Birmingham wasn't and isn't a very rich area. It was rather dreadful and everybody in my family worked in factories, really mindless jobs that were physically exhausting. My dad thought I should become a tradesman, to get a chance and better myself, get away from the factories. I tried to become a plumber. It didn't work out; it wasn't for me. Then I tried to become a bricklayer. It didn't work out. Then I tried to be a construction worker—same story. Everything I tried seemed to be doomed."

(New York Rock, 2002)

"Shortly before I left school, the Beatles got popular and they were my first addiction. I could switch off, forget my surroundings, and dive into the music. It was something magical, almost a spiritual experience for me. Of course, my dad hated it."

(New York Rock, 2002)

"The Beatles were revolutionaries and their music was revolutionary music. You know, they were considered to be a bad influence because they gave the kids ideas, the ideas to do something else with their lives than waste it in factories or become plumbers. For adults, it was a dangerous thing. But for us, they were heroes."

(New York Rock, 2002)

"I would sit for hours daydreaming —wouldn't it be great if Paul McCartney married my sister?' You know when there's a certain song on the radio and you think, 'I remember dating that girl,' or whatever. You're thrown back into that tune, the smell, the aura of that time. It was a very enlightening part of my life, and the Beatles were a big part of it. They started my dream rolling. And how I got from that to Black Sabbath I don't know."

(Observer, 2007)

"I used to do some crazy things. I was quite yappy, really. When I was 18, I nicked some stuff, a load of woman's clothing. I was going around selling stockings in the pubs. Eighteen years old, they caught me and I went to prison. That's where I got all tattooed. I did it to pass the time in prison with a needle and India ink."

(Rolling Stone, 1971)

"I'm a lunatic! I went through a shop window, fighting with three guys. My arm was virtually fucking ripped apart. I was on a glucose drip for twelve hours, had several pints of blood pumped into me. I'd just gotten out of prison...burglary."

(1982)

"I was 17 and pissed off and I wanted to see the world and shoot as many people as possible—which is not much different from being in a band these days, the rap world anyway."

—On wanting to join the army (Mojo, 2000)

"How far did I get? About three feet across the fucking front door. They just told me to fuck off. He said, 'We want subjects, not objects.' I had long hair, a water-tap on a string around my neck for jewelry, I was wearing a pajama shirt for a jacket, my ass was hanging out and I hadn't had a bath for months."

—On trying to join the army (Mojo, 2000)

"For years my mother would say, 'When are you going to pack up this rock 'n' roll nonsense and get a proper job.' And my dad would say, 'You've got to learn a trade'—he was a toolmaker. I thought joining the army would please him."

(Mojo, 2000)

**"If you haven't got your own mind
and can't do what you want, you're not
an individual, just part of a mass."**

(1972)

**"The society trip in England is that you
go to school, then get a job, and at the age of
twenty-one you get married. You work the rest
of your life in a factory and when you retire at the
age of sixty-five you get a gold watch; forty-five
years in a factory with stinking oil, polluting the
land. I used to work in a factory and I used to
see these blokes dying on their machines.
That just blew my mind."**

(1972)

**"I've been dictating [my autobiography]
to my son, who's helping me on his computer.
I'm spending a lot of time doing research.
I've just got up to 1971, when I went crazy
and dived through the window. My life is
so full of interesting stories..."**

(Launch.com, 2/11/2000)

"On January 20, Nineteen Seventy-fucking eight, my father died. The fucking ironical thing about the whole deal was—he was fucked, he had like cancer from his throat, what's this tube down to your stomach? Esophagus, testicles; he was riddled with it—he died in the same hospital that my daughter was born seven years prior. My daughter was born 11:20 on January 20th, and my fucking father died seven years later in the same hospital at 11:23 on the 20th. It was fucking weird, man."

(1982)

"When they go, they're out of their misery. But what freaked me out more than anything else was the funeral. I was singing fucking 'Paranoid' in the church... Seconal, drunk... it blew me away. All the family came that I'd never seen for fucking years, and they were making comments. In England, it's a weird scene at a fucking death."

(1982)

Chapter 2

Sabbath Bloody Sabbath

Everybody knows the Black Sabbath story. They're the band fronted by the guy who bites the heads off bats and doves. They're the band that worshipped their devil, whose singer landed his own reality show. He's criminally insane, they are inherently evil and, between them, their music has driven their own fans to suicide.

At least, that's what the tabloids say. The reality, of course, is somewhat different, although forty years after Black Sabbath launched their career—and gave birth to the heavy metal genre that still dominates the modern rock landscape—that reality has often been both purposefully and inadvertently obscured, by the band, by their audience, and by the modern media's perception of the entire package.

In late 1967, Ozzy teamed with three friends, Geezer Butler, Tony Iommi, and Bill Ward, in a band called Polka Tulk, and prepared to join the wild ferment of local talent thrusting its way into the public eye. The Moody Blues and the Move had already put Birmingham on the rock 'n' roll map; now they were being joined by a host of new groups, including Robert Plant's Band of Joy, Christine McVie's Chicken Shack, Denny Laine's Electric String Band, Jeff Lynne's Idle Race, and many more.

Polka Tulk became Earth became Black Sabbath, and attracted the attention of independent producer Tony Hall, who secured them a record contract with the Fontana label. After just one single, the group was transferred to the sister Vertigo label, a newly formed company specializing in progressive rock. *Black Sabbath*, the band's debut album, was released the following February, among the first Vertigo label releases. Months later, they scored their first hit single. In October 1970, following the band's first American tour, "Paranoid" reached No. 3 on the UK chart (No. 61 in America), and established Black Sabbath at the forefront of the now burgeoning heavy-metal boom.

Black Sabbath remained among rock's premier attractions for the next five years, their popularity only flagging as the band's own energies began to dissipate. The blur of live and studio work that the group undertook during this period—they recorded an album a year, and undertook five world tours—is rivaled, according to rock legend, only by the tempest of sex and drugs that accompanied the rock 'n' roll.

But Black Sabbath was also plagued by business difficulties, and a series of financial and tax-related misdoings that plunged all four members into serious difficulties. It was in a last-ditch attempt to release themselves from the grasp of the multitude of sharks feeding from the band that Black Sabbath finally aligned themselves with one of the biggest sharks of them all, legendary manager Don Arden.

The stories told about Arden are both legion and, as history has proven, extraordinarily litigious. Alongside fellow 1970s entrepreneurs, Led Zeppelin's Peter Grant, David Bowie's Tony DeFries, and the Beatles/Stones' Allen Klein, he developed a reputation of near-untouchability.

What nobody—least of all the members of Black Sabbath, as they passed through his office and nodded to his 18-year-old receptionist daughter, Sharon—expected was that the great man was teaching her everything he knew…and then some.

Although their recruitment to Arden's managerial stable promised to breathe new life into Black Sabbath's increasingly exhausted body, the realities of the group's continued existence did not change. Two final albums (the latter marked by an utterly unexpected UK hit single, "Never Say Die") prefaced the end; a last American tour, during which they were absolutely upstaged by the supporting Van Halen, confirmed it.

Osbourne was sacked by Black Sabbath in 1977, immediately before work began on the final album. He was replaced briefly by fellow Birmingham vocalist Dave Walker, and then by American Ronnie James Dio.

DISCOGRAPHY

BLACK SABBATH (1970)
PARANOID (1971)
MASTER OF REALITY (1971)
VOLUME FOUR (1972)
SABBATH BLOODY SABBATH (1974)
SABOTAGE (1975)
WE SOLD OUR SOUL FOR ROCK 'N' ROLL (COMPILATION; 1976)
TECHNICAL ECSTASY (1976)
NEVER SAY DIE (1978)
LIVE EVIL (RECORDED, 1975; LIVE, 1982)
REUNION (LIVE, 1998)
SYMPTOM OF THE UNIVERSE (COMPILATION, 2002)
BLACK BOX (BOX SET, 2004)
GREATEST HITS 1970–1798 (2006)

❝The reason Black Sabbath evolved was this: at the time we were fucking doing it...we wanted to be successful; we wanted to be rich. We wanted to get out of that fucking shithole we were living. We were originally called Earth, and we thought, 'What do people really love to fucking hear? What do people really want, 'Sugar sugar sugar, trying, true true true,' and all this fucking lot coming out your radio?' I'm thinking I've got no shoes on my feet. I'm walking around in fucking rags. I said to the guys, 'Listen, man—there's so many fucking people out there, talking how wonderful the fucking world is, and there's so many of us fuckers that ain't got nothing.'❞

(1982)

❝We never consciously knew what
we were doing: we were just four innocent
guys—very awkward and very unorthodox—
who played what we were feeling, trying
to make ourselves feel good.**❞**

*— On what it is about his band's music that
has made it last so well (Independent, 1996)*

❝My mother said to me, 'Get a proper job.
Quit this fucking around.' She still thinks it's
a crazy fucking thing I'm doing.**❞**

❝We were living in Birmingham. No shoes on my feet. And I
thought, 'This shit is for the rest of my life.' I put the radio
on, and there's some guy, 'If you go to San Francisco, be sure
to wear a flower in your hair.' And I thought, 'This is bollocks,
the only flower I'm likely to wear is on my fucking grave.'**❞**

(Observer 2007)

❝Frank Zappa, who was a very techno guy, invited us to a
restaurant once where he was having a party. He said, 'The
song "Supernaut" is my favorite track of all time.' I couldn't
believe it. I thought, 'This guy's taking the piss: there's
got to be a camera here somewhere...'**❞**

"I used to play in a band called Rarebreed, but the guitarist really annoyed me. Tony, Bill, and Geezer were playing in bands, but they kind of split around the same time and that is how we all came together. It was really funny; I vaguely knew Tony. We went to the same school, but he was older than I am. One day I went into a record store and put up a sign saying 'Ozzy Zig seeks gig.' I used to call myself Ozzy Zig because I thought it sounded cool and I thought everybody would start asking who Ozzy Zig was. Anyway, Tony showed up and I thought he'd think I'm a complete idiot, but he ended up joining our band."

(New York Rock, 2002)

"We started off playing jazz and blues. Cream, Fleetwood Mac, John Mayall's Bluesbreakers, the Beatles, and Jethro Tull were our influences. At one point, we had a bottleneck-guitar player and a saxophone player."

(Rolling Stone, 2004)

"You go on stage and see 15 people in the circle battering each other to pieces. We've still gotta try and say, 'We love you,' with this guy lying on the floor with a bottle sticking out of his throat."

(Melody Maker, 1975)

"I once went to a fortune teller, and she said that I would have a thousand pounds in the bank by the time I was twenty-one...and that I would be a very famous person. At the age of twenty-two, I had a thousand pounds in the bank—excess of—and I was getting success. It wasn't planned. I don't know what the fucking hell's happening to me."

(1982)

"We told our friend Alvin Lee from Ten Years After that we'd changed our name to Black Sabbath, and he says, 'You won't go very far called that.'"

(Rolling Stone, 2004)

"The early days with Black Sabbath were the best years of my life, and when we get together we always talk about those days. You know, remember when you OD'ed?"

"I was the guy who used to get all the shit and eat all the chocolate. I remember once we were down to our last ten pence and we went, 'What shall we get? Four bags of chips or ten No6 tips? Fuck it, we'll get the fags."

(Music Toob, 2009)

"We recorded the first album on our way to catch a ferry. The manager goes, 'Just stop off for the day and record them fuckin' songs you've been playing.' It was fucking primitive: Two four-track machines in a studio smaller than this room! Twelve hours later, we were finished. It was like, 'Wow, I thought recording records would be a lot harder.' "

(Rolling Stone, 2004)

✝

"I remember when the first Black Sabbath album came out I thought, 'Great, I can show my dad.' We put it on the old radiogram and I remember him looking at mum with this really confused look on his face and turning to me and saying, 'Son, are you sure you're just drinking the occasional beer?' "

(Mojo, 2000)

"I suppose we are similar to Grand Funk Railroad, but I hadn't heard of them until our third tour here. We didn't realize how big they really were until we played the Forum with them and they just packed the place—two nights! They turned the crowd on, but musically they didn't do anything for me. I'm not saying they're a bum group, because they've gotta be a good group for people to dig them. Personally, I like to hear music which is considerably different than what we play."

(1972)

66We'd finished recording (second album, *Paranoid*) already when we wrote 'Paranoid.' That song came about when our producer told us to jam for four minutes. I came up with the vocal line, Tony came up with the riff, and Geezer came up with the lyric. It was done within an hour. If I couldn't create a great vocal melody, I would just sing along in unison to the riff, like on 'Iron Man.' It was the easiest solution— I wanted to get the fucking thing done.99

(Rolling Stone, 2004)

66We thought, 'Let's scare the whole fucking planet with music.' 99

66When someone identifies with the downer song that I'm singing, they're able to put their energies into the music and relieve their frustrations. It's good therapy. If I make people feel good, I feel good. The band and the crowd gets off on each other and it's a tremendous trip: Peace Power. I don't wanna see people get busted on the head. I've been through that whole trip, been knifed a couple times, and it's not much fun.99

(1972)

"Well, you know, people describe us sometimes as if we ran around fields with pitchforks in our hands. I think they expected flames to shoot out of the cover of our second album. Want some Doritos?"

(Circus, 1972)

"The trouble with English and European crowds, is that they listen to you as if you were a jukebox. They shove in their 14 bob, or whatever it is, and expect you to work your balls off. What I dig about America is if you do a duff gig because you're worn out through traveling and you're not into it, they still dig it because they're into your trip."

(Disc, 1972)

"It's every British band's dream to play the States. When we got there finally, we fucked as many groupies as we could. In San Francisco, they even had a Black Sabbath parade! Coming from Birmingham, England, where the fuckin' sun never shines, it was magic to us."

(Rolling Stone, 2004)

"What I dislike about studios is you've got a 24-track desk and this monster of a machine to screw around with. I hate studios. It's like being in an incubator for six months.**"**

(1978)

"When we did (the *Volume Four* album), it was like one big Roman orgy—we'd be in the Jacuzzi all day doing coke, and every now and then we'd get up to do a song.**"**

(Guitar World, 2000)

"One night me and Bill were fucking drunk and taking a piss together. I see this aerosol can and squirt his dick with it. He starts screaming and falls down. I look at the can and it says, WARNING: DO NOT SPRAY ON SKIN—HIGHLY TOXIC. I poisoned Bill through his dick!**"**

(Rolling Stone, 2004)

Ozzy and Tony rock out during the Live Aid concert in Philadelphia, PA., in 1985.

"There's one thing that everybody has got to understand about Black Sabbath's lyrics. They're not downer lyrics. They're just telling everybody where it's at. People must think we sleep off the rafters with wings on our backs every night, taking reds and drinking wine. We're just people."

(Melody Maker, 1975)

"Sabbath were a hippy band. We were into peace."

"In the seventies with Sabbath, if I'd had a crystal ball that said you would be hailed into the nineties, and the next century, I wouldn't have believed it. I didn't for a long time anyway. I thought people were taking the piss with that 'I'm not worthy' stuff."

(Observer, 2007)

"Black Sabbath had the same members all the time and that was boring. That was the thing with Sabbath—we all wanted to split, but we didn't know where to split, how to split. I certainly didn't know how to audition people. What do I know about good guitar players or drummers or whatever? I just sing."

(Creem, 1986)

"We all thought we were tin gods. But at the end of the day it just turned round and kicked us in the teeth. I just want a simple life for a while. I just want to be an ordinary, everyday, run-of-the-mill guy. Inside I ain't a tin god. I ain't a tin of beans walking around. And that's what I began to feel like: a product. 'Buy Ozzy Osbourne and he'll clean your carpet faster than anything else.'"

(NME, 1977)

"(The Rock And Roll Hall of Fame)…Just take our name off the list. …The nomination is meaningless, because it's not voted on by the fans…"

"The end of Sabbath and me (was) because they went in a fucking macho way, and I never. They went sort of like, 'We ain't gonna do this, we want five towels, we want fuckin' eight bars of soap, we want fucking Courvoisier,' all this shit. It was bollocks to me, because I still remember my roots, where they never."

(1982)

"I want to write a book. It's going to be all the fun we had…not."

(1979)

CHAPTER 3

THE PRINCE OF DARKNESS

aybe it was simply the increased media surveillance, maybe there really was an explosion of occult activity across the western world around the time that Black Sabbath were born. But the Age of Aquarius that had been so warmly welcomed in song, dance, and counter-culture cliché also seemed to be reawakening sensibilities that society had kept buried for over 200 years.

The Manson murders in August 1969 were simply the most high profile; the Zodiac killings in San Francisco that same season merely the most perplexing. Across America, Britain, Western Europe, witchcraft apparently lay at the root of everything, from horrific murders to brutal church and cemetery desecrations, from missing children to messy divorces. All of which, apparently, were on the increase.

In the face of such sensationalism, so much of it driven by speculative assumption or simply opportunistic criminality, the true nature of what is so readily tagged "witchcraft" wasn't simply overlooked; it was lost altogether. Even when no actual wrong-doing was involved, the press of the day reveled in the so-called "confessions" of both white and black magicians, gleeful accounts of wild orgies and secret ceremonies, the involvement of well-known celebrities and highly placed politicians. Hammer's 1972 horror potboiler, *The Satanic Rites of Dracula*, in which vampire hunter Van Helsing stumbles upon an evil plot whose sponsors are drawn from the uppermost echelons of government, could have been drawn wholly from the headlines of the previous three years.

The more salacious revelations were not afraid to name names either. The high priests of devil rock were Rolling Stones Mick Jagger and Keith Richards, of course. But, cavorting demonically among the hordes of familiars who flocked to their cloven feet, were "the newly formed midlands pop group" Black Sabbath.

Black Sabbath themselves studied the maelstrom gathering around them with increasing bewilderment but not, of course, without some satisfaction. It was another Stones' associate, former manager Andrew Loog Oldham, who pronounced that, when a band is first starting out, all publicity is good publicity and, no matter who Black Sabbath's audience was, nor why they were drawn into the band's orbit, there was no denying that the group's reputation was a powerful draw.

Today, Geezer Butler—the band's primary lyricist—laughs off that reputation. The only devils that the group ever signed a pact with were the businessmen whose own machinations would, ultimately, so benight the band's career. And the only sacrifices that took place in their dressing room were the band members' own sense of self, as the industry machine took over the men and drove Black Sabbath into the ground.

He admitted, however, to having at least a passing familiarity with the world into which Black Sabbath were moving. "I was brought up an incredibly strict Catholic, and I believed in Hell and the Devil. But, though I'd been taught about God and Jesus, no one ever went into what the Devil was all about. So, when I was 16 or 17, around 1965, 1966, I went about trying to find out."

His experimentation never went beyond reading what we might as well term the "required literature," with Aleister Crowley and Dennis Wheatley at the top of the list; and toying with a few half-hearted, and absolutely unsuccessful, incantations and spells. Nothing dramatic, nothing life-changing, nothing to shatter the other faiths that he held.

But, as with all teenaged experiences and experimentations, what he read and learned remained with him—and, he continued, "because I wrote most of Black Sabbath's lyrics, some of that ended up in the songs. But it was never advocating Satanism. It was warning people against evil."

Those intentions, of course, remained well hidden in the face of all the supposition now swirling around the band; so well hidden that it wasn't simply the gutter press that missed the meanings in Black Sabbath's songs. Their core audience, too, could not see the woods for the trees.

Black Sabbath was still an unknown infant when, at the end of an especially evocative Birmingham show, a young woman appeared in their dressing room—nobody actually saw her walk into the room, suddenly she was just there—and introduced herself as the head of a local coven. She wanted Black Sabbath to perform at their next gathering, to welcome the Dark Lord with their hymns to His glory. The group's musical energies, coupled with the coven members' own mental powers, would ensure a successful outcome.

It was not the first time the group had been invited along to such an event and it would not be the last. So, they gave her the same response that they gave everybody else: a polite refusal followed, once she had left the room, by an exchange of raised eyebrows and disbelieving guffaws. Where do these nutcases come from?

Except there was something about this particular nutcase that disturbed them, an intensity to her bearing, a strength in her eyes, a firmness to her voice. If she was mad, or deluded, or simply winding them up, she'd obviously been practicing for a long time. Neither, though they never saw her again, did she seem at all happy about having to take "no" for an answer.

Over the next few nights, the band members experienced strange dreams, odd coincidences, a general feeling that something was not quite right, and more. And—though there was nothing any of them could actually put their finger on and explain, even the dreams were forgotten upon waking, with only a kernel of disquiet to even prove they had happened—it was impossible to shake the sensation that something had happened. Or, was about to.

There was something else going on as well, something that Ozzy finally put into words a few fraught days after that now ominous visit. "Do you get the feeling that everybody else knows something that we don't?" His bandmates were stunned, but not necessarily surprised when, after dropping Osbourne off at his parents' home that same evening, his father came to the door to see them off. He said goodbye, then his voice lowered a little. "You'll make sure you look after Big Ozz, won't you?" The next day, Ozzy turned up at rehearsal carrying four aluminum crosses, one for each of the band members. His father had made them during down time at the tool plant. Without a word, all four looped the chains around their necks.

THE DEVIL GETS ALL THE BEST TUNES: SATAN'S TOP TEN

"AFTER FOREVER"
"BARK AT THE MOON"
"BLACK SABBATH"
"CHILDREN OF THE GRAVE"
"DEVIL'S DAUGHTER (HOLY WAR)"
"HELLRAISER"
"MR CROWLEY"
"SIN"
"THE ULTIMATE SIN"
"ZOMBIE STOMP"

" I believe in a power greater than myself. I don't think of God as some white haired old fucker sitting on a cloud... God? Stuck another O in there and that's what I believe in. Good. **"**

" I feel like I've met (Aleister Crowley). I feel that I was a servant of his once. **"**

(Circus, 1980)

" The only black magic Sabbath ever got into was a box of chocolates. **"**

" I'm just a rock and roll rebel, I tell you no lies, they say I worship the devil, they must be stupid or blind. God, beam me up! **"**

"If I kill myself doing what I do for a living, if people want to fuck me up, say whatever they like, it's their privilege—it's your privilege. But I don't think I do a bad job; I don't think I fucking give people harm. What's more fucking harmful than a simple guy like me that's got an ability to fucking turn people on, to have a good time, to go crazy? What the fuck's wrong with—what's more crazy—giving a young kid a fucking rifle and saying, 'Run over that fucking hill and you're gonna die,' or me getting up there and jumping ape end down like a c**t for an hour and a half?**"**

(1982)

❝I mention the word 'death.' I mention the word 'evil,' but in the context of the story—it's like 'Mary had a little lamb.' They all think I'm singing, 'Satan, Satan, Satan, Satan… death, murder, murder.' They think that's all that comes out of my mouth. They never stop to listen. They've already prejudged me and tried me, and I ain't gonna sit there trying to defend myself. Anybody that knows Ozzy Osbourne, and knows what I'm about, knows me anyway. And if doing what I'm doing is wrong, I'm sorry.❞

(Spin, 1986)

❝I was born in fear and I've got many, many demons that affect me on many, many levels…❞

❝When (*The Exorcist*) first came out in the '70s, I can remember going to the movie theater in Philadelphia with Black Sabbath. And Black Sabbath is, of course, this satanic band of rock and roll—and yet we were that scared that we all spent the night in the same room. Up until that point it had been strings and fishing lines when the bat flies out, but that one was so real.❞

"How can a four-foot midget sing about the devil?"
— *On Ronnie James Dio joining Black Sabbath*

"Geezer wondered if it was a bit too heavy when he wrote, 'Would you like to see the pope on the end of a rope?' in 'After Forever' (from *Master of Reality*); Geezer's Catholic, you know. You remember that guy from New York, Son of Sam, who was killing all the chicks? When they got into his apartment, he supposedly had the lyrics to 'After Forever' written on his wall. I thought, 'Fuck me, are we going too far?'"
(Rolling Stone, 2004)

"I have tried to read the Bible but I'm dyslexic. I was stuck on Genesis for three fucking years."

Ozzy and his son, Louis (from his first marriage), at a cover shoot for the album, *Diary of a Madman*.

"Yeah. This geezer came at me with a sword
on stage once but me road manager bashed him
with a mike stand. Another time this geezer came
up all distressed and said, 'Hey man, I've been
trying black magic and it didn't work, what
do you advise?' I said, 'Try Milk Tray'"

(Sounds, 1981)

"I mean all this Bible burning, we used
to do that in fucking '71! Just to have
something to do! We'd get drunk and burn
the Gideon's Bible in the hotel room!"

"I'm not a Prince of Darkness grandfather.
They call me Granddad Ozzy."

(Observer, 2007)

"I'm a Christian. I was christened as a Christian.
I used to go to Sunday school. I never took much
interest in it because…I didn't. My idea of heaven
is feeling good. A place where people are all right to
each other. This world scares the shit out of me."

(Spin, 1986)

"I don't want to sit around with my finger
up my ass praying to some hole in the sky."

(Sounds, 1981)

"We're all living on the tinderbox. It's like
there's some maniac somewhere trying to devise
a new means of destruction. It always amazes
me that mankind always goes to find the biggest,
powerfullest means of destruction before they find
anything good. It's always the negative things
they find first. Since I've had kids I've thought,
'What are we leaving these people? Nothing.'
What a future we've got for mankind."

(Spin, 1986)

"I don't believe in God as a physical thing sat somewhere on a cloud in heaven. I reckon heaven and hell are what we make of life right here on earth. I don't believe in the afterlife. I think when you die you're just simply like a piece of shit that needs flushing away."

"I'm the Prince of Darkness, not fucking Neil Young!"

(Rolling Stone, 2000)

"I really wish I knew why I've done some of the things I've done over the years. Sometimes I think that I'm possessed by some outside spirit. A few years ago, I was convinced of that. I thought I truly was possessed by the devil. I remember sitting through *The Exorcist* a dozen times, saying to myself, 'Yeah, I can relate to that.'"

(Hit Parader, 1984)

"To me, it was always theatrical. I've never practiced black magic. Do I look like a fucking black magic practitioner? I collect fucking art, I've got Toulouse-Lautrec and the fucking Three Graces over there. A clown doesn't go home and watch telly with his red nose on. He's a normal bloke. I'm not the same person offstage as onstage. But when I was doing alcohol and drugs, I was becoming that person. And it was such hard work."

(Uncut, 1997)

"People don't really know how black my Sabbath was over the years."

(NME, 1977)

"Rock and roll is my religion, and that's the God's honest truth. And it's my law."

(1982)

CHAPTER 4

THE MAN WHO INVENTED HEAVY METAL

n the beginning, there was...the Riff. And it was loud, skull shatteringly so. The Kinks knew this, so they wrote, "You Really Got Me." The Who knew it, too, so they wrote, "I Can't Explain." The Yardbirds, Cream, Jimi Hendrix, Vanilla Fudge, Blue Cheer... rock archaeologists have spent three decades trying to figure out who to blame for what became heavy metal; rock critics have spent just as long trying to cure it. But when the evening's young and the beer's a-flowing, still nothing gets the party rockin' like a dose of dat ol' devil music boogie, and a cat with no ears could map out the parameters.

Blue Oyster Cult – *On Your Feet Or On Your Knees*
The title says it all, and the fact that it needed two stuffed LPs to accommodate the full majesty of a primal mid-seventies BOC live show adds a deafening addenda. Recorded a full year before "Don't Fear the Reaper" launched the band into grown-up moms and dads-flavored AOR metal; at a time when Patti Smith could be proud of dating the keyboard player, and "7 Screaming Diz-Busters" really meant something profound, *On Your Feet* also includes the definitive version of "Born To Be Wild"—think a menopausal Motörhead in a really foul mood.

Deep Purple – *Machine Head*

According to bassist Roger Glover, "Smoke on the Water" was originally called "Title #1," and almost never made it onto the album. Good job it did—if any song could ever define a band, or the genre that they helped to dominate, then "Smoke" defines Deep Purple, and the rest of *Machine Head* as well. But it's chockablockagoodstuff regardless, with "Lazy," "Maybe I'm a Leo," "Pictures of Home," and "Space Truckin'" just stacked up like a pile of B-sides behind it. So, an essential metal album? Maybe not. But the world's longest, greatest, heaviest 12-inch single? Could be.

Grand Funk Railroad – *We're An American Band*

Which wasn't actually much to boast about in 1973, but they did it anyway, and with a damned sight more panache than most of what else was crawling round the heartland back then. The key to the album was the swaggering "Walk Like a Man," a beer-bellied, napalm-belching wake-up call to all those nancy bands who wore make-up and high heels. Like KISS, probably. Or maybe the Carpenters.

Kiss - *Alive*

Nobody bought a KISS record because they liked the music. People bought KISS records for the same reasons they send money to those "adopt-a-starving-orphan" appeals on late-night television. Because whoever could resist a band which looked like that? Big eyes, big tongues, exploding guitars, levitating drummers—KISS could have been the most god-awful cacophony of sludge-laden macho riffola on the planet, and they'd still have sold a million trillion. Which is just as well, because that's precisely what they were.

Led Zeppelin – *II*

Their first album invented blues rock, their third invented folk, the fourth was stuck with "Stairway to Heaven," and the rest were too clever for their own damned good. But *Zeppelin II* was heavy, man, and that was just the parts which weren't even heavier. "Whole Lotta Love," of course, dominates the show; "Heartbreaker" and "Livin' Lovin' Maid" keep the heads a-banging, and then you get to the lasciviously leering "Lemon Song," all about juices running down Robert Plant's legs. They can cure that nowadays, you know.

All of which is very nice. But really, if you genuinely want to know what heavy metal was, is, and forever will be, look no further than this baby:

Black Sabbath - *Paranoid*
If you only own one Sabbath album, make sure this is it. And if you only want one metal album, this is it as well. Everything is here, from the stadium-rocking anthem ("Paranoid") to the droning atmospheric lull ("Planet Caravan"), from socio-political comment ("War Pigs") to the brainless riff from hell ("Iron Man"), Ozzy at his screamiest best, and the band doing their Sunday best impersonation of Panzers on the White House lawn. The final track is called "Fairies Wear Boots." And they're still stomping on your head when the record ends.

The Greatest Riffs on Earth

"Children of the Grave"
"Into the Void"
"Iron Man"
"NIB"
"Paranoid"
"Sabbath Bloody Sabbath"
"Snowblind"
"Supernaut"
"Tomorrow's Dream"
"War Pigs"

"Black Sabbath was a back-street band—
like the punk thing, if you like. I'm not saying
we were before punk, but in our own way we were
what the punk groups are now: a people's band.
I don't want to play it, but I'm into the new wave
because you don't have to be a brain surgeon to
listen to it. It's just a simple, down-to-earth
music that people can tap out on a tin lid."

(NME, 1977)

✝

"It's become trendy for bands to say they're
influenced by Black Sabbath. When I started
with Sabbath, the music scene was soul, blues,
pop, psychedelic, and the flower-power movement.
Now us guys, living in the fucking dregs of Aston
in Birmingham, no money, no shoes on your feet
and we're hearing on the radio, 'If you go to San
Francisco/Be sure to wear some flowers in your
hair,' and we're thinking, 'What the fuck's that all
about?' Now, we used to rehearse opposite a movie
theatre and Tony Iommi said, 'Isn't it funny that
people pay money to be scared by horror films?
Why don't we start writing scary music?'
And that was how it all began."

(Uncut, 1991)

"We see a lot and we write about what we see. We have a couple of songs about people getting stoned, but so have a lot of people. It's a heavy, doomy thing but it's what we see. A love thing wouldn't go with the style of music we play. It's like going to see *Frankenstein* with *The Sound of Music* soundtrack behind it. It wouldn't go."

(Melody Maker, 1975)

"I really don't feel like the father of metal or rock, more like a big brother."

(New York Rock, 2002)

"I'm really not proud of everybody who claims to be a fan and thinks I influenced them. I remember some terrible '80s pop bands who considered me their inspiration. By chance we were playing the same festival and that guy Limahl (singer with '80s one hit wonders Kajagoogoo) wanted me to sign all his (Black Sabbath) albums. I told him to get lost and that I wanted no part of his music and no responsibility for his taste in music. Well, you can pick your nose, but you can't pick your fans."

(New York Rock, 2002)

"People call us 'downer rock': you take the reds, man, and drink the wine and blow out, get high on the decibels; all that's a lot of rubbish. Whatever people do at our concerts is none of our business as long as they enjoy it. I'm just out to entertain people— a good old show business trip."

(1972)

"I didn't invent that form of music. When I look back now at that song, 'Black Sabbath,' I think, 'How the fuck did I even begin to think of a melody like that?' I don't know how to do it any more. I think it was like a combination of my Beatles' melody thing combined with those blues bands at the time—John Mayall, Fleetwood Mac, and Savoy Brown. People say I invented that music but it wasn't me. I was part of a band called Black Sabbath, there were four of us and we all had our say."

(Sunday Times, 2005)

"I used to like anything that was heavy. The Kinks' 'You Really Got Me' did something to me, and I use to dig the early Who and Led Zeppelin. I dig anything that makes the hairs in the middle of my spine stand up. We just started writing our own stuff and our sound just evolved into what it is today—it wasn't planned."

(1972)

You can't do a video game celebrating classic heavy metal without involving the man, who, along with his band, Black Sabbath, is credited for inventing the genre. In the comedic action-combat video game, *Brutal Legend*, about a demon-fighting super roadie named Eddie (voiced by actor Jack Black), Ozzy plays the Guardian of Metal, who aids Eddie. It was reported that both Black and Ozzy frequently injected profanity into their scripted lines during recording sessions, which led to the inclusion of an option of a profanity content filter to bleep out the bad words. Ozzy has been praised for his work in the game.

❝I like to do a song that two people will hear differently. I write two songs about nuclear disarmament, and everyone in America goes, 'So Ozzy how come you've got serious?' I write a ballad, and everyone goes, 'What are you doing? You sound like ELO on acid.' It's really difficult working in heavy metal: if you do anything off the track, they jump on you like a pile of bricks.**❞**

(NME, 1986)

❝The biggest thing has been realizing how much people really do love the early Sabbath music. I remember years ago when Metallica opened up for me, I went backstage and they were playing old Black Sabbath albums and I thought they were taking the piss! They said, 'No, we really love Sabbath.' I couldn't see that at the time, because towards the end of my time with Sabbath 20 years ago, I thought what we were doing was boring and stupid, because we were boring and stupid, totally sick of what we were doing and totally out of our brains with drink or drugs when we were playing it.**❞**

(Launch.com, 2000)

"Our music is aggressive, people can get off on it. It gives them a release. I can see it happen at concerts. We get people's aggressions out. Then they won't go out and beat some old lady over the head. It works for me, too. Like when I'm at home for a while, not working, with no outlet for me energy, my wife and I are hammer and tongs at each other cause I'm all pent up. But our music gets it out, for me as well as the audience."

(Rolling Stone, 1971)

✝

"I miss the lack of melody (in current music) as well. A lot of people think I'm crazy for liking Creed and I like them purely because they sing! I mean, the singer of Creed sings like the guy from Pearl Jam, very close kind of voice. But I like the fact that Creed sing. I don't care if they're a Bible band, Satan band..."

(MTV.com, 2002)

"If you were to see a heavy metal crowd, they do tend to intimidate, what with their tattoos and piercings. And you're always going to have some people there that are extreme in their behavior."

(2001)

❝I really like Motörhead. I can dig where they're at—they don't want no shit, they just go out and blow their asses off and they've been going down great every night.❞

(Sounds, 1981)

❝Dimebag (Darrell) was a dear friend of mine. I'm absolutely beside myself with grief. I can't for the life of me understand why someone would do this. Pantera toured with me many, many times.❞

In response to Darrell Lance Abbott being shot and murdered on stage in 2004 while performing with his band, Damageplan

❝When we started writing things we didn't want to present bullshit like, 'I'm gonna see my chick and we're gonna get it on.' It's all hypocritical. Let's face it, you only remember the good times because you don't wanna remember the bad. You can have a whole month of downer and only one good night and you'll remember the good night. If you feel positive, that's fine, but we wanted to write things the way they really were. Geezer furnishes most of the lyrics.❞

(1972)

"All that stuff about heavy metal and hard rock, I don't subscribe to any of that. It's all just music. The heavy metal from the seventies sounds nothing like the stuff from the eighties, and that sounds nothing like the stuff from the nineties. Who's to say what is and isn't a certain type of music?"

(Guitar World, 2000)

"I kept hearing that metal is dead and Ozzy's dead and people that like Ozzy are dead. I have never had an empty seat. I've always sold out, so who's saying it's all over?"

(cnn.com, 1998)

"I always hear that whole 'metal is dead' crap. The truth of the matter is that when we started the Ozzfest, media-wise, yes, metal was dead. But as far as the kids went, it was still huge. It was just that radio and MTV decided it wasn't in vogue with what they wanted to do at the time, so the average person didn't hear too much about it. That's why when it comes to picking the new acts each summer, we have people out there on the Internet and in the clubs looking for good music and finding bands that people are excited about. I want to know what the kids are into, because I don't trust the industry."

(Guitar World, 2000)

CHAPTER 5

WAR PIGS

 ar Pigs," the opening cut on Black Sabbath's second album, *Paranoid*, is regarded by many as the archetypal Sabbath song. Well, that and "Black Sabbath" and "Paranoid" and "Iron Man"…

They certainly thought so; right up until the last minute, the album itself was going to be titled *Warpiggers*, and the porcine warriors that still prance across its cover are a reminder of that. But then the group wrote "Paranoid" itself, a hit single beckoned, and the label changed the album's title.

No big deal. "War Pigs" remains the leviathan that flavored the rest of the disc. It is also the closest the band ever came to overt political commentary in any of their songs. Inspired by the then (1970) ongoing conflict in Vietnam, but looking back, too, over the centuries of conflict that had already occurred, the message of "War Pigs" is both chilling and simplistic. It is not the citizens of a nation that starts a war. It is the politicians who won't actually have to go out and fight it. "They," sang Ozzy, "leave that all to the poor."

It is a topic that Ozzy has returned to on many occasions—probably because it's a subject that our leaders, too, have returned to with wearying regularity. From the ruined landscapes of Ozzy's own childhood to those that flash across our television screens every time we switch on the world news; from Margaret Thatcher's vainglorious campaign in the Falklands in 1982, to George Bush's still current invasion of Iraq two decades later, there has barely been a year when one or another of the countries Ozzy has called home, the UK and the US, has not been either rattling, or waving, its saber at somebody. And if you add to that the years of abject terror which were foisted upon us by the propaganda machines of the Cold War—another twenty-year span during which every day could be doomsday—then the message of "War Pigs" comes home even harder. Every time another bullet is fired, or another tank gets bogged down in a trap, a rich man gets a little richer.

No wonder we're always finding someone else to fight.

"I don't understand war. If you're on one side, and I'm on the other, and you get killed and I get killed, we've both lost. I'd have thought people would have learned, humanity would have learned."

(Observer, 2007)

"If hell is worse than this place, then those of us going to hell are on a hard ride down, baby. Hell, to me, is nuclear holocaust. It's the biggest fear I have as a man. It worries the pants off me that we're all going to blow ourselves to shit. And it will happen, I believe. I can see it will happen. I asked my old drummer Tommy, 'Do you think they'll use the atom bomb?' And he said, 'Ozzy, they've never made a gun that hasn't been fired in anger. 'I thought, 'Shit that's right, man.'"

(Spin, 1986)

"Weather in Afghanistan, 2,000 degrees and cloudy. What the fuck am I doing? I'm stuck on the weather channel. AHHH!"

"They say military have the so-called 'secret intelligence'—this amount of intelligence must be very secret, since I've never seen any intelligent military person, nor I have seen any sense in the bloody stupid wars."

"It's a fucking terrorist, man! It's fucking part of Bin Laden's gang!"

"We can't even educate people about the dangers of nuclear war. Over here there's fallout shelters everywhere. Who's got 'em in Britain? The politicians and the very few. What about us? It's about time people started to question the government. All we'll get is an HM Government Warning—this bomb may seriously damage your health."

(Sounds, 1981)

❝I'd rather have people get rid of their aggression at an Ozzy concert than by beating some old lady over the head and running off with her purse. It's a release of aggression. It's built-in aggression. Why do they get young people to join the army? Because an older guy thinks, 'Fuck you! I'm not going over that hill. You think I'm crazy?' And a young guy will go, 'Yeah! Let's go get 'em.'❞

(Spin, 1986)

❝Have you seen *They Saved Hitler's Brain*? Oh you've got to see that one! Hitler's brain is like this goldfish bowl in the back of a Nazi limousine in South America and it's giving out orders to all these Nazis. It's so hokey! And in the end it self-destructs itself.❞

(2001)

❝(Tony Blair) came up to me at an awards ceremony and said: 'I used to be in a rock and roll band, you know, but I could never get the chords to 'Iron Man' right.' And I thought to myself: there are kids dying in Africa and our own boys are going off to war and you're talking to me about 'Iron Man?'❞

(Telegraph, 2009)

"I'm comfortable. I'm crazy—totally crazy, and the fact is accepting my craziness. I'm totally fucking freaked by every man, your universe, and everybody, because everyone's gone fucking mad... They say I'm crazy—I am crazy, okay? But I don't fucking build bombs, I don't build fucking means of killing people. All I do when I get to a concert is try and give them my best shot. Sometimes it works, sometimes it don't. A lot of times, it don't."

(1982)

"He plays those war games, my son, and I'm a World War II buff."

"Politicians are scumbags. They're all fucked. What about the people? The fucking mass unemployment? I'll tell ya, I predict a bloody revolution over there. People say I've got power over people, I should make a stand, but that's not up to me... Don't get me wrong, I'm not a Communist, far from it, there's just got to be a better way of living."

(Sounds, 1981)

CHAPTER 6

STONED IMMACULATE

It has been said, and not without a degree of accuracy, that the only way to become a truly successful rock 'n' roll star is to first master the arts of excessive drug abuse, excessive alcoholic consumption and, if you're still standing at the end of that, excessive excess of every other variety. Or to act like you have.

But it is a sad reminder of how deep political correctness has infiltrated modern society that, today, even rock's most legendarily dissolute icons look back on their legendary pasts and shake their heads sadly, as if to deny that they ever were as drugged as they usually appeared to be.

Not because they're ashamed of it (well, not necessarily), nor even because they're genuinely sorry. They deny it because rock 'n' roll has developed a conscience and doesn't want to unduly influence an impressionable younger generation.

Kids look up to their parents' old heroes today, and it doesn't matter that that was one thing those parents never had the opportunity to do—because it's hard to look up at someone when they're crashed out in the corner. When somebody can seriously place hand on heart and swear, "It really wasn't as bad as it looked back then," you know that rock 'n' roll hasn't simply lost its teeth. It's lost its soul as well, and even the devil has given up trying.

Bow down and genuflect before Ozzy, then. He doesn't simply remember his past. He honors it as well, and the only caveat he might offer is the one that used to open the old *Superman* TV show. Ozzy could fly. You can't.

"I only wanted one drink every time I went out the door but I had 9,000. I thought I was having the greatest time of my life and used to think I was the craziest guy in rock 'n' roll but you know what? Even crazy people want a rest."

(MusicToob, 2009)

"The lifestyle I've been living for the last 30 years, I could have been dead a thousand times."

"There were these horses in a field. They were talking to me."

"I was 18 when Sony offered us a deal for Black Sabbath. £105 they gave me—and I'd never seen so much cash in my fucking life. From then onwards, I could get drunk morning, noon, and night, and nobody would care. There isn't another job in the world where you can turn up pissed as a wheel and not get fired."

(Telegraph, 2009)

"With me, it was the longer the bus journey, the more I could get fucked up. I would drink until I dropped, do coke, LSD, anything."

(Observer, 2007)

"I once tried transcendental meditation, but I got fed up and smoked a joint."

(Observer, 2007)

✝

"I'm quite sane now, but I won't be sane for long, after I take this pill. Metrospan, they're called. They really give you a hit on the head. A doctor gave them to me for depression a few days ago. They must have some ups in them; they make me crazy."

(Rolling Stone, 1971)

"I'm a fucking hypochondriac, I am. If I feel anything wrong with my body, I go straight to the doctor. I know I have a drink problem. I've been told that if I don't stop drinking as excessively as I am drinking, my liver's going to pop off. That's the risk I fucking take. I understand it. I know."

(1982)

"I was hung up on cocaine for years;
I took LSD, me and Bill Ward took LSD for two
years every day. I ended up a screwball. I got to
this lunatic asylum and this guy says to me, first
question: 'Do you masturbate?' I turned to this
guy and I says, 'Listen, asshole, I'm here for my
head, not my cock.' But I've read about it since.
I don't read a lot. I've read about it since, and
apparently masturbation for guys is a very big
sign of insecurity, which I am—I'm very
insecure. Within myself. It's true."

(1982)

"There was a period when
I could not fucking walk."

(Mojo)

"My son said, 'Have you seen these old interviews
with you, Dad?' And I went, 'No, I can't stand to
watch.' I'm so pathetically fucking drunk. It's like
watching a fucking train wreck or something."

(MusicToob, 2009)

"(Black Sabbath) didn't touch hard drugs for a while, we used to drink and smoke pot and do a few pills. Then we discovered cocaine. It was like bullshit powder. You think you are bigger than you are. It amplifies your ego while you're on it. Then it starts to get hold of you. We got all fucked up on cocaine. I tried heroin a couple of times but it didn't agree with me. When I first snorted cocaine I thought, fucking hell, this is what I've been waiting for all my life, it's the best feeling I've ever had. But then you're forever chasing that first feeling and you never get that again."

(Sunday Times, 2005)

"I've done a lot worse than jump off piers, son. Like throw a television out the window."

"I am a raging alcoholic and a raging addict and I didn't want to see my kids do the same thing."

"If I were to say to a kid, 'I'm going to put you in a candy shop, I'm going to close the door, and you're not allowed anything.' Soon as that guy buggered off, it would be, 'I'll just try a bag of that.'"

(Observer, 2007)

"(I took my first driving test) about 1974, then '75, '76, '77, '78. I've lost count how many times. I remember one time I was doing the three-point turn and I passed out because I'd been to the doctor's earlier and got some Valium for my nerves. At the end they'd say, 'You've failed,' and I'd be staggering around the car park. Some (examiners) would say, 'I'm not even fooling getting in the car with you.' Would you?"

(Independent, 2009)

"You don't have to take a drug to be a monster! It's pathetic what I was like. On that *Bark at the Moon* tour I was insane. I didn't know what I was doing. I couldn't remember anything. Talk about blackouts! And the most horrific thoughts would come to mind. If a cop came up to me and said, 'I'm arresting you for the murder of so-and-so,' I wouldn't know. And I said no, this has got to stop, I'm losing control here. It's one thing getting pissed and falling on the floor, but when you don't have a clue what you did yesterday...I'd have had to give my wife a video camera to follow me around and show me what I was up to!"

(Creem, 1986)

"I've been pissed out of my face, chased people with a shotgun, driven fucking Range Rovers over viaducts and come out without a scratch."

(MusicToob, 2009)

"What the hell's wrong with getting fucked up?"

(1978)

"I blew tons of fucking dough on things I'd broken and paying people off not to sue me. And I thought, 'Keith Moon died, so-and-so died, I must be next.' And I still didn't stop even though I knew I was dying."

(Uncut, 1997)

"I knew I was in trouble when I couldn't make it offstage quick enough to get whatever variety of shit I was tipping down me. I thought to myself: There are people working in gas stations, and all these menial jobs, to put money aside to see the Ozzfest, and I'm more interested in going back to the hotel, and doing a bag of white powder, or whatever shit it is I'm on."

In 1986, Ozzy announced he was giving up drugs and drink, although he admitted he was still having trouble with the latter.

"I'd get arrested more times than I didn't. I'd go to the doctor for a medical and they'd call up my wife and say, 'Listen, we've got some pretty alarming news for you. Don't plan on having a long life with your husband because his liver's about to fly out of his asshole.'"

(Uncut, 1997)

"I don't want to be the next Elvis Presley, Keith Moon, or Jimi Hendrix. I'm content with the ordinary things in life, like going to pubs and drinking beer. Why should I take Ozzy off stage and walk the streets with him? No thanks, he's fucking barmy."

(Sounds, 1980)

"It was my biggest fucking fear. I always feared going out and getting fucked up and having somebody say, 'That's the guy that killed my son.' I was having blackouts and doing crazy shit. I didn't even know what the fuck I'd done. I'd wake up in different beds with different people and think, fuck, what am I doing here?"

"I turned my 15-year-old (Elliott) on to fucking marijuana. I said to him, 'Son, I'd prefer you to smoke this than tobacco.' He says, 'Why, Daddy?' I says, 'Because you can't physically smoke as many cigarettes of marijuana as you can of tobacco, because tobacco is the subtle drug of all.' Because you don't realize... You smoke a big fat joint and you're dead—you're crashed."

(1982)

"I have this little demon that keeps making me drink."

"I was always a miserable drunk."

(Uncut, 1997)

"I always drank alcoholically. I never drank socially. I always drank to get pissed as a fart. It's like spending the day banging your head on the wall and at the end of the day you've got this big lump on your head and you're thinking, 'Fuck me, what is the fucking point?' And then you wake up and start banging your head on the wall all over again."

(Uncut, 1997)

"One day, I'd just done a line and was feeling really hot. I pressed this button on the wall thinking it was the air conditioner—instead, it alerted the police! All these cop cars show up, so I go into the toilet with all the drugs, trying to do them all before they came in!"

(Rolling Stone, 2004)

"We were lying on the beach sunning ourselves where the tide was some way out and there was a tall lookout tower for the purposes of a life-guard with a diving board. Suddenly this hippy gets off the ground and starts climbing the ladder with a glazed look in his eye. No one really believed he was going to do it but he did, dived straight off this ten-foot-high board into beach! He got up, scratched his head and wandered off, still stoned out of his crust!"

(Record Mirror, 1971)

"For the best coke, just ring three-eight-nine-oh-nine-eight, only one hundred dollars!"

(1972)

"What Sharon would do to try to stop me drinking was take my clothes. So if I wanted to get a drink I'd have to dress up in hers. I was alone in my hotel room in San Antonio and I wanted the hair of the dog, so I put one of her dresses on. I'm walking around the town with this green evening gown on, slurping from a bottle of Courvoisier, drunk as an idiot, and I want to take a piss, so I see this old wall and I think, 'This'll do,' but unfortunately it's the Alamo."

(Independent, 1995)

"This stuff is so strong you don't have to smoke it. Just stick your head in that bag and sniff."

(1989)

"I can honestly say, all the bad things that ever happened to me were directly, directly attributed to drugs and alcohol. I mean, I would never urinate at the Alamo at nine o'clock in the morning dressed in a woman's evening dress sober."

(MTV News Online, 1992)

"I became a blackout drinker about a year ago, as far as I know. I may have been one for many years and never realized it."

(1989)

"I'd get up in the fucking night and drink! The last house I had, this beautiful 400-year-old house in Buckinghamshire, the only reason I bought it was because at one end of the lane was a pub I could go to without getting done for drunk driving, and at the other end was an old geezer who brewed his own wine which was like fucking loony soup, y'know?"

(Uncut, 1997)

"We've all gone out and had a few drinks and woken up next to this person who you don't even know where you've met her from, y'know, and I didn't want to do that. I didn't wanna wake up in a strange place with some strange people or end up in some toilet sniffing coke all night. I felt like a fucking sewer rat."

(Uncut, 1997)

"One time we had a kids' party, one of the kids' birthdays, and Sharon said to me, 'You fucking should have seen yourself yesterday,' and I went, 'What's wrong with me, I was all right, playing with the kids, whatever.' And she kept saying, 'Do you want to see yourself?' and she put a video in the machine and I was fucking freaked out. I thought, 'Maybe it's true.' "

(Scotland On Sunday, 2009)

"It wasn't as if I had a list. I didn't have a resumé saying, Tuesday—have a pint, strangle the wife; Wednesday—get bail."

"Drugs were making me miserable. They weren't working. I'd get high and come straight back down again, then do it all over again."

(Mojo)

"I go mad on booze. I just love drinking and getting drunk. I'll drink anything. I'm the Dean Martin of heavy metal..."

(Melody Maker)

"I suddenly realized that when I was a drug addict, I used to write things like 'Flying High Again,' 'Snowblind,' all this shit. And the other night, I thought, 'Fucking 'ell, I sing one song for it and then straight after I sing one song against it.' But the thing is, that's OK. Because that was where I was when I wrote that, so why shouldn't I do it? It's part of my life. It's a part of what I am and what I will be."

(Spin, 1986)

"I might start singing fucking religious songs. I don't think so, but if I choose to, why not? To think that you can't sing stuff from your last album because now you're a different man is bullshit. If they're good enough to write and good enough to hear and to buy, then they're good enough to sing onstage, you know? I'm not ashamed of anything that I've done in the past."

(Spin, 1986)

"Some people never stop. Like when George Best died, he had fucking liver transplants, the whole nine yards, and he still continued to drink. Alcohol, drugs, tobacco, it's all the same, it's something to fix the way you feel, but it started to turn on me."

(Scotland On Sunday, 2009)

"As time went on my tolerance got bad, I could hardly hold anything. I'd drink and then have to have another drink to get me back up again, so by nine in the morning I was done. That was when I used to have a sniff of the old powder and get me back on my feet again. At first it was fun to do, but then it became not fun anymore and I had to do that just to get to what I thought was normal. I'm becoming awake again now, you know?"

(Scotland On Sunday, 2009)

"My scam was pain pills. I'd tell them my L4 and L5 lumbar were out of whack and there's no way of disproving that it is or isn't, so they give you pills."

"I'd have a bag of weed and a fridge full of beer and lock myself in a room and do nothing but drink myself into a stupor."

"Rehabs are not there to cure you. You'll never get cured from addiction, but they'll tell you what's wrong and suggest how you can arrest the symptoms. It's a terrible affliction and thank God people have recognized it as being an illness."

(Scotland On Sunday, 2009)

"If it wasn't for Sharon, I'd be long dead. Sharon would go fucking insane at me. The last thing you want is someone yelling at you when you're doing coke or drugs. She didn't do fucking aspirin. She tried to keep up with the drinking but then we were in Monmouthshire where we used to rent a farmhouse to rehearse. We had a fucking heavy night. Next morning she said she was so sick she'd never touch the stuff again. Now she just has the occasional glass of wine."

(Sunday Times, 2005)

"I've gotten to the point in my life that I cannot fucking do it any more, because... I suppose it's maturity or something, I suppose."

(1982)

"When you're a kid of fucking 24 or 25 and you come from Aston to the States and you see all these fucking c***s wanting to be fucked, you go like a bull at the gate. You're like a fucking lunatic. I was having perverted scenes, fucking...all kinds of crap was going on with my sexual life. It's bizarre, it was wild. It fucked me up at the end, because my biggest dread is getting a disease I can't get rid of, and there's a lot of diseases that you can't get rid of."

(1982)

"I choose to fucking keep myself to myself. It may sound a little bizarre, but I choose to keep myself to myself. I'm a moody bastard, because I want people around me, but I don't."

(1982)

"If I had done everything they said I've done, I'd be dead."

"I never thought I'd see the day when I'd be getting fucking excited over a cup of tea."

CHAPTER 7

RIDING THE CRAZY TRAIN

n early 1979, his will to continue crushed by drug and alcohol problems, Ozzy was finally, and irrevocably, sacked by his bandmates. They replaced him with former Rainbow vocalist Ronnie James Dio and, over the next two years, a rejuvenated Black Sabbath effortlessly rode a new tide of support created by the recently born new wave of British heavy metal.

There never was any question whether Ozzy Osbourne would launch a solo career; the equation that nobody could answer was, whether he would actually be able to sustain it. Certainly Sharon Arden had her doubts, although she furiously shouted down the general industry view that Ozzy was washed up.

Indeed, when Black Sabbath's record label made it clear that it had no interest whatsoever in retaining his services as a solo act, it was Sharon who persuaded her father to sign him to his own Jet label; and when Arden senior announced that he, in turn, was no longer interested in managing Black Sabbath, she ensured that Osbourne did remain on the family books.

A professional relationship was slowly blossoming into romance, although there was still some way to go before either Sharon or Osbourne were able to relax enough to enjoy it.

Instead, the next few years saw their lives devoted to the creation of a myth, via the creation of the bat-biting, bird-beheading, Alamo-defacing, suicide-suggesting media image that would come to define Ozzy in the public eye.

He witnessed tragedy, when guitarist Randy Rhoads was killed in a plane crash during a tour; and controversy, after the parents of a suicidal teenager blamed one of Osbourne's songs for inciting the boy to take his own life. But new albums, live appearances, and one outrage after another kept Ozzy's name alive through the 1980s, and only once did he seem to slip, when his highly publicized 1991 resolution to finally quit touring—his "farewell" outing was even titled No More Tours—proved highly premature. Within three years, he was back on the road, this time touring under the banner "Retirement Sucks."

That tour completely reinvigorated Ozzy. Over the next three years, he threw himself back into his work, not only maintaining his own recording career, but also working with, among others, metal stars Lita Ford and Steve Vai, alternative act Therapy, comedian Billy Connolly, boxer Frank Bruno, and Muppet Miss Piggy.

In 1996, the Osbournes launched the first in what has since become one of the most successful summer festival tours of all time, Ozzfest; the following year, the couple formed their own record label, naturally named Ozz Records. Osbourne's own career, too, continued to soar. In 1997, he reunited with Geezer Butler and Tony Iommi to headline the second Ozzfest tour; by 1998, fellow founding member Bill Ward, too, was back on board and a full scale Black Sabbath reunion tour was underway. And today, he remains Ozzy Inviolate, riding the crazy train to the end of the line.

OZZY OSBOURNE DISCOGRAPHY

THE BLIZZARD OF OZ (1981)
DIARY OF A MADMAN (1981)
SPEAK OF THE DEVIL (LIVE, 1982)
BARK AT THE MOON (1983)
THE ULTIMATE SIN (1986)
TRIBUTE (LIVE, 1987)
NO REST FOR THE WICKED (1988)
BEST OF OZZ (COMPILATION, 1989)
TEN COMMANDMENTS (COMPILATION, 1990)
NO MORE TEARS (1991) – 4 MILLION COPIES SOLD
LIVE AND LOUD (LIVE, 1993)
OZZMOSIS (1995)
THE OZZMAN COMETH (COMPILATION, 1997)
DOWN TO EARTH (2001)
LIVE AT BUDOKAN (LIVE, 2002)
THE ESSENTIAL OZZY OSBOURNE (COMPILATION, 2003)
UNDER COVER (COMPILATION, 2005)
PRINCE OF DARKNESS (BOX SET, 2005)
BLACK RAIN (2007)
SCREAM (2010)

"I have a saying. 'Never judge a book by its cover.' I say that because I don't even know who Ozzy is. I wake up a new person every day. But if you've got a fantasy of Ozzy, who am I to say? I mean, if you think I sleep upside-down in the rafters and fly around at night and bite people's throats out, then that's your thing.**"**

(Rolling Stone Online, May 1997)

"It's more a money thing now. I'm going to make as much money as I can, then shoot myself.**"**
(Rolling Stone, 1978)

"When I left Sabbath I was in total fucking turmoil in the mind. I thought I'd blown the biggest thing in my life, the only one crack I'd ever get out of the fucking suburban shithole. I'd gone to Los Angeles and auditioned so many Tony Iommi look-alikes, it was untrue. At the end of the day, this guy said, 'I want you to listen to the guitar player.' I was stoned out of my face, as usual. Heard one guy at 4:00 in the morning, and he was only tuning his guitar when I said, 'You've got the gig.' Phenomenal.**"**
— On hiring Randy Rhoads (1982)

"I wanted to make music that I know people could relate to. Who knows about martians? Has anyone ever seen a martian? Well then what are we writing about martians for? The whole reason I pulled out of Sabbath was I didn't feel I was giving the people my heart.**"**
(1982)

"I've yet to do a concept album, and I want to do a concept album. Every track feeds into the next, you know? That's the idea I have. Whether it comes off or not, I don't know."

(1982)

"The other day, I went to a chiropractor. He's just a regular chiropractor. Whenever I meet someone who doesn't know me, they say, 'Oh you're the guy who bites the heads off everything.' I get kind of cheesed off with it, but at least they remember. The thing that pisses me off is that that's not what I'm about. If that's what you think Ozzy Osbourne's about, then you're way off."

(Launch.com, 1998)

"I'm not particularly a happy person."

(Hit Parader, 2000)

"...if the crowd starts to thin, diminish, then I'll see it as a sign that it's time to hang up my microphone. I don't want to go from arenas to bars, you know?"

— On retirement (Goldmine, 2010)

"I'm easily manipulated, and I hate to feel I'm
letting people down. And a lot of people use it against
me. I say I don't wanna do something, and then I think,
'Ozzy, are you getting a big head?' I always remember
the time I had nothing and it wasn't so long ago,
Sabbath doing gigs to pay lawyers' fees. I'm not short
by any means, but there's always another gig. It's like
a boxer: like an addiction, you can never say no. I'm a
very excessive man. I don't feel I've done it unless
I'm lying in hospital with a drip sticking out my
arm...hey, man, what a great tour!**"**

(NME, 1986)

"Why are they trying to tag it on us guys?
To be Ozzy Osbourne, you got to be somebody special.
Because they hit you with so much shit...if you were
soft anywhere, if you were susceptible, a magnet for
emotion, you'd be dead. And I cannot no way take no
responsibility for some guy who puts a gun to his head.
A guy in New York a few months ago got a big
tax demand, and he couldn't pay it, and he jumped
out the window of a 50-story apartment. What
does his wife do? Sue the government!**"**

(Spin, 1986)

"Some fans have issues and they make you the focus of their craziness. They'll say, 'I told you not to wear the red shirt.'"

(Mojo)

"They're telling me I'm putting ideas of people shooting themselves in their heads. I was watching MTV the other day, and there was a band come on called the Pet Shop Boys, and you want to hear the opening lyrics of that song? 'There's a madman in town/Put a gun to your head/Pull the trigger.' Something like that. I thought, 'My god, that's probably going right over their heads, but if it was Ozzy Osbourne singing that song, I'd have fuckin' pilgrims down at the hotel in a minute."

(Spin, 1986)

"They were suing me for having subliminal messages, backwards-tracking stuff. It takes me all my time to do it the right way. I mean, it wouldn't be a very good career move if everyone who bought my records killed themselves, would it?"

(Observer, 2007)

"I've now been sued by about 25 people who claim their kids committed suicide from listening to my music."

(1997)

"I don't know about you, but if I went home tonight and found my kid lying face down in the bath with a suicide note saying, 'Goodbye Dad, I'm off,' and a New Kids on the Block album was playing on his stereo, the last thing on my mind would be suing the group. I'd be grief-stricken."

(Independent, 1996)

"I did put a backwards message on one of my records in the end. It said, 'Your mother sells whelks in Hull.' That really freaked them out in the Bible Belt."

(Uncut, 1997)

"I live at night more than the day. I travel through the night. It keeps me out of trouble."

(Spin, 1986)

"If we stay in the town after the gig, it's crazy. A photographer from your magazine came to the show last night, and he was white with fear at the end of the show...I've noticed a hell of a lot of violence and destructiveness from the people. I don't know if it's the changing of time or what. When we did the Meadowlands, there was $172,000 worth of damage to the hall. I remember different tours from different incidents. But there seems to be a hell of a lot of tension in the people now."

(Spin, 1986)

"I'm the original clown. When I was a child at school, if people were miserable around me, I'd do some crazy things like jump through fucking doorways, anything to make them amused—hang myself, anything—because I hate to see sad faces."

(1982)

"I must be one of the most sanest people you ever met, because I'm insecure, I'm nuts, but I know that I'm here. I believe that I'm here for a purpose. I believe in forces of fate. It must sound like a pile of shit to you."

(1982)

"I fell in love with Randy as a player and a person the instant I saw him. He had the best smile in the world. Randy was the best guy in the world to work with. There is no comparison between him and Tony Iommi, and I can only compare the two because they were the only guitar players I had ever worked with. I was attracted to Randy's angelic attitude towards the whole business. I didn't have to teach him anything; all that he was lacking was guidance. He listened to every word I spoke to him, and we had a great rapport together."

"Had he lived, I truly believe he'd have been one of the greatest guitar players that ever walked the earth. He was when he was here."

"I have no regrets except that I wasn't up to keep Randy from getting on that plane."

(Guitar World, 2000)

"Don Airey deserves a George Cross. He went into the house that was on fire to try and save someone. Our bus was just 20 feet from the explosion. If the plane had been a couple of inches lower, the whole lot would have gone up. I could feel the bastard tip up. The only consolation was that it all happened so quickly, they didn't suffer. But it was such a tragic loss."

At right: Ozzy and Randy Rhoads. Rhoads was killed on March 19, 1982, when the small plane he was on crashed into a mansion. He was 25. The pilot and another passenger were also killed.

❝I sang for the Queen of England, met the president of the United States, and got an Emmy and a star on the Walk of Fame. And what did I do? I was just being myself.**❞**

❝I'm not a musician—I'm a ham.**❞**
(1982)

❝I like to write things of interest. We've all heard of boy meets girl, shoves his dick in her and goes home... Whitesnake are always writing about snake's dicks, lizards, slide it in, up and down, and backwards. There's more interesting things than shoving your dick. We've all heard them, we've all got them and we've all done it; you get a shaking leg and you go to sleep. It's so fuckin' obvious.**❞**
(NME, 1986)

❝I'm a total split personality. I just do the best I can. I've never had any ambitions to be a great singer. I'm just happy to act like a lunatic on stage.**❞**
(Sounds, 1980)

❝I advise that pregnant women
do not come to my concerts.❞

❝There's not a stupidest thing. I've dressed
in women's clothes, I've dressed as a Nazi. I've
gone onstage naked. I've gone on so drunk I didn't
even know I did a show. I've done so many
stupid things, but it's all part of Ozzy.❞

(Launch.com, 1998)

❝I never pre-planned 99.9 percent of the things
I've done. Some were drastically wrong, some
were drastically right. I don't know if you saw
the VH1 thing (VH1's *Behind The Music* Ozzy
documentary) recently. In one hour, it's
impossible to write my life down.❞

(Launch.com, 1998)

❝What is this? ... It's music
to get a brain seizure by.❞

“I'm confused by it all. I look at myself
and think, 'Have I changed that much?
Am I really so special?' I don't understand.”

(Classic Rock, 2004)

“I'm one of these guys, I wake up in
the morning and got a fucking problem:
I'm looking for something to kill or blow
up or some fucking thing.”

(Rolling Stone, 2002)

“I have a message for anyone coming to the
Ozzfest this summer. If you're planning to jump
up onstage during my set, please do not give me
any bear hugs, because they fucking hurt. Listen
to me, I'm dead serious. On the first night of last
year's tour, this enormous guy jumped up onstage
and gave me a huge bear hug. He crushed three of
my ribs and I had to do the whole tour in absolute
agony. I couldn't believe it, the first fucking show!”

(Guitar World, 2000)

"I don't consider myself a great singer, but I have a connection with the audience. There's the artist, and then a void and the audience; but I like to be part of the audience. I'd like to be them, and I'd like them to be me for an hour and a half. I get criticized for being the antichrist, causing kids to commit suicide, but that's total bullshit. My intentions are not that."

(Launch.com, 2003)

"I get to my early 50s and, all of a sudden, I'm this sort of worldwide figure. It was a weird transformation and I still don't feel so great about it."

(Classic Rock, 2004)

"Of all the things I've lost, I miss my mind the most."

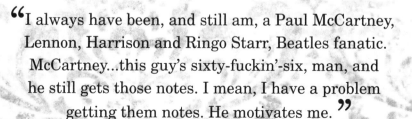

"I always have been, and still am, a Paul McCartney, Lennon, Harrison and Ringo Starr, Beatles fanatic. McCartney...this guy's sixty-fuckin'-six, man, and he still gets those notes. I mean, I have a problem getting them notes. He motivates me."

(Goldmine, 2010)

"The down side of being outrageous is that you have to go around explaining your fucking self to people. If you're too cocky, somebody might just pull out a fucking gun and cock it and blow your fucking face off. You gotta be really careful what you bite off. Don't bite off more than you can chew. It's a dangerous world."

(Rolling Stone Online, 1997)

✝

"I've had thousands of death threats."

(Independent, 1996)

"I've had numerous threats on my life. They were gonna shoot me one night. I go to this gig and there's this strange vibe going down backstage and all of a sudden this cop walks in and goes, 'We've had it from a very good source that this guy's gonna try and shoot you tonight, what do you want to do?' I went, 'Well, they're in so if I don't go on they're gonna get fucking pissed off. They're not gonna shoot me when I'm onstage, I don't think.' I thought I'd just move around a bit more, use Tony my assistant as a shield."

(Scotland On Sunday, 2009)

"I remember one time on tour in the Midwest, we got to the hotel at six in the morning and the next morning I'm wanting a doctor for me throat. And I'm in the coffee shop waiting for him, and this straight-looking guy comes in in a suit and I get up to greet him, thinking he's the doctor. Someone in a suit and tie started screaming, 'Put Jesus in front of you' and all the other people in the restaurant turned out to be with him, so they all joined in. Then this Rambo guy who's with me goes into kill mode and starts throwing them all through the window. I had to crawl out of there literally on my hands and knees."

(Independent, 1996)

"They're trying to sue me in California about this kid who shot himself. It says in this one line, 'Breaking laws, locking doors, but there's no one at home/Make your bed, rest your head, but you lie there and moan/Where to hide? Suicide is the only way out,' or something. But that's one paragraph in the song, and the song is about alcoholism. The danger of alcohol. A certain percentage of alcoholics can't stand it anymore, and they jump off a fucking building... But the press picks up on one line in a song and keeps shoving it down people's throats. They're saying this fucking song forced this kid to shoot himself. The kid was fucking well sick in the mind long before he ever heard an Ozzy Osbourne record."

(Spin, 1986)

"Every year they have Halloween, and all I do is take Halloween night out on the road every night. It's like a Halloween party every night. If that was the case on Halloween night, the police cells would be full. Everyone would have turned satanic for the night!"

(Launch.com, 2003)

Ozzy appears at news conference in Los Angeles on Jan. 21, 1986, to explain that his song, "Suicide Solution," was misinterpreted and is actually anti-suicide. The parents of a teenager who shot himself blamed the song for inciting the boy to take his own life.

"I go for the melody. One thing I got from The Beatles: they always had great, great melodies and great harmonies. You're like, 'What the fuck is that about?' But it fits the song, you know."

(Goldmine, 2010)

"I have a genuine love affair with my audience. When I'm on stage, they're not privileged to see me. It's a privilege for me to see them."

✝

"One night in Hamburg, I painted my face purple, and didn't realize it was indelible. So I had to walk around Hamburg for the next three days with a purple head!"

🤘

"I'm spoiled. I've had so much good luck happen to me that I can't handle bad luck. It's very hard to explain to you, but I've had a lot of bad luck lately. As much good luck as I've had, I've had bad luck. But the good luck, it goes in a pitch. It rises like a dam—as much good luck as I get, I get as much bad luck. So you—gotta fucking work it out in my own head."

(1982)

"You get some complete nutters. I had this guy rang me up from Texas all the time. First of all, the guy said I was his father—fucking hell, he was nearly as old as me! Then he sent me a photo of this tomb that he'd built, and he said he fully believed I was gonna go down to this place and spend the rest of eternity with him. And I said to my secretary, 'Don't ever wind this guy up because he might turn out to be another Mark Chapman or something.'"

(Uncut, 1997)

"Sharon told me the box set was coming out whether I liked it or not."

(Mojo)

"I'm not the greatest singer in the world, but I do give people entertainment."

"I find it hard to write about boy meets girl and they fall out and the rain comes down and the sun shines and they're up in the cloud of bullshit."

(Goldmine, 2010)

"Let me explain something to you; you have not been standing in front of thirty thousand decibels for thirty-five years—write me a note!"

"Sometimes I'm scared of being Ozzy Osbourne. But it could have been worse. I could have been Sting."

"There is something fucking unbelievable about seeing all of the fans go crazy and chanting, 'Ozzy!' I would pay to see them."

(askmen.com, 2002)

"If I was about to bite the head off a bat now, would people give a fuck? Remember (Sixties American singer) P J Proby when his nuts fell out on stage? They could walk on stage now with no gear on. When something's been done, it's been done."

(Independent, 2009)

"All I ever wanted was for people to come to my concerts and have a good time. I don't want anyone to harm themselves in any way, shape, or form—and my intentions are good whether people want to believe it or not. I'm not going to suddenly become a Jesus freak or anything. But I do have my beliefs and my beliefs are certainly not satanic.**"**

(Rolling Stone Online, May 1997)

"One of my greatest regrets is that I urinated on the Alamo.**"**

"(My new album, *Scream*) is very heavy. It's a cross between—it's kind of like a Sabbath/Ozzy album, you know. It's kind of, it wasn't meant to, I didn't plan on doing it but that's the way it unfolded. A lot of it's very, very heavy. I love it.**"**

(Noisecreep, 2010)

"Sharon. This looks very dangerous to me. This looks like I'm on tour for the next nine years.**"**

CHAPTER 8

ANIMAL WELFARE

 zzy has always maintained a wary existence around our two-, four- and multi-legged friends. He must have, otherwise why would he have stabbed, shot, or bitten so many?

"I shot a cat once for shitting on my car. The cat cost 35p and the car cost six grand—no contest."
(Sounds, 1981)

❝I spent three years in a slaughterhouse, killing cows and pigs and all sorts of things. It got pretty bizarre. I was figuring out all these different ways to kill these animals. Have you ever drank blood? Ox blood, pig's blood. I have, and I gotta admit, the first time you do it, you get quite a weird feeling. You kinda stick a knife in there and hold out your cup. After that I got into the habit and started drinking it rather frequently.❞

(Oui, 1982)

❝The final straw was when I shot all our cats. We had about seventeen of them and I shot them all. My (first) wife (Thelma) found me under the piano in a white suit, holding a shotgun in one hand and a knife in the other.❞

(Daily Mirror)

❝The bat thought I was giving him the kiss of life!❞

❝Sometimes I think my whole career and life has only been about a bloody bat!❞

"It took a lot of water to down just that fucking bat's head, let me tell you. It's still stuck in my fucking throat, after all these years. People all over the world say, 'You're the guy who kills creatures? You still do it? You do it every night?' It happened fucking once, for Christ's sake."

(Rolling Stone Online, May 1997)

"Dogs smoke in France."

"I got rabies shots for biting the head off a bat but that's OK—the bat had to get Ozzy shots."

"I'd like to learn to juggle cats on stage, see how that goes down."

(Sounds, 1982)

"It's like Dr. Doolittle in this fucking house here."

Ozzy, Sharon, and one of their many dogs, Maggie, a Japanese Chin.

**"You don't need to hire a dog therapist,
you just need to wake up at 7 a.m.
and open the fucking door!"**

"If people would only look at the situation...
I've been in this business 15 years and if they
realized the shit I have to go through for my name
to be remembered... I was at a CBS convention,
right? You don't realize what these business things
are like. All the old codgers are there and they don't
give a fuck about you, it's just a sham. They play
your album while you're there then forget you. Well,
I wanted to make a real impression. The scam is
the bird was dead. We were planning to release it
there, but it died beforehand. So rather than waste
it I bit its head off. You should have seen their faces.
They all went white. They were speechless. That
girl in the pictures was screaming. Eventually a
bloke came up and said 'You better go. What did it
taste like?' It tasted warm, like tomato sauce.
Next time it'll be a piranha fish."

(Sounds, 1981)

"The dove's head landed on the PR chick's lap
in a splatter of blood. To be honest with you,
I was so pissed, it just tasted of Cointreau. Well,
Cointreau and feathers. And a bit of beak."

(I Am Ozzy, 2009)

"It's amazing people remember all the crap; but it's not anyone's fault but mine, and the amount of mileage I've had out of it has been amazing. It just gets a bit tedious when someone goes, 'So Ozzy, tell me, what do bats taste like?' The amount of times I've been asked that question in America— 'Now we have the infamous bat-biting rock 'n' roll freak, Ozzy Osbourne!' Sideshow, sideshow...I tell 'em it tastes like a good McDonalds. Jack and Jill went up the hill..."

(NME, 1986)

"I bit the head off a live bat the other night. It was like eating a Crunchie wrapped in chamois leather."

"Y'know what I'd like to do? I'd like to open up a restaurant and every time someone ordered a steak, I'd bring a live cow in and slaughter it in front of them."

(Sounds, 1981)

"I'm gonna start on parrots next, at least they can say 'no, no' as my teeth close in.**"**

(Sounds, 1982)

"Fish like cheese, sometimes. Sometimes some fish like cheese.**"**

"They still picket the gigs, they still try to ban me. One night—this is how crazy they are—I'd been traveling on a bus for seven hours, and we stop at a truck stop in the middle of nowhere. This guy comes in at seven in the morning, and he hands me a piece of paper, saying, 'Read this, Jesus loves you.' And I say, 'Where did you come from?' And he says, 'I've been following you all night' And I'm thinking, 'You must be out of your fucking tree. Go help a homeless person.' We've had police roadblocks stopping the bus and threatening us—then one time I turned on the radio and there was a message flashed to all farmers. 'Do not sell any animals to any stranger because he might be Ozzy Osbourne.' **"**

(Uncut, 1997)

CHAPTER 9

LOVE, MARRIAGE, AND BRINGING UP BABY

They say that behind every great man, there is a great woman. Twice-married Ozzy could also add half a dozen children to that equation, three (one adopted) by his first wife, Thelma Riley, the remainder from his thirty-year marriage to manager, Sharon.

Ozzy met Thelma while she was working in the cloak room at a Birmingham club called the Rum Runner...later to find fame as the venue where Duran Duran was discovered a decade later. The two moved in together and married shortly before Ozzy left for Black Sabbath's first American tour in 1971. It was not, Ozzy has since revealed, an especially happy marriage. In his autobiography, *I Am Ozzy*, he claims they remained together for as long as they did (they finally divorced in 1982) for the sake of their children, Jessica and Louis, and Thelma's son, Elliot, whom he adopted.

He had already fallen in love with Sharon by then; they would marry in Maui, Hawaii, on July 4, 1982, and have three children, Aimee (born on Sept. 2, 1983), Kelly (born on Oct. 27, 1984) and Jack (born on Nov. 8, 1985). Kelly and Jack would both rise to fame as co-stars of *The Osbournes* MTV reality show; Aimee refused to have anything to do with it.

"Sharon is my manager as well as my wife, and she's steered me in the right direction up to now, as you know."

(Classic Rock, 2004)

"I don't think anyone is totally happy; you can't really wake up in the morning free of hassles and do what you want as long as you don't harm anybody else. If you wanna stick needles into your arm it's your own life. Like, I'm not into taking heavy dope although I have taken dope. People who take it just have hang-ups that they can't deal with."

(1972)

"My father never set me down and told me the facts of life, sex, the dangers of alcohol, tobacco, whatever. And I've survived a lot of alcohol and drug abuse so it's my duty to sit my son down and say things like, 'If you're going to have sex, don't go out in the rain without a rain coat. Wear protection. Don't be stupid.'"

(2001)

"Sex is as natural as breathing. But I'll tell you, I wouldn't want to be a teenager these days with the HIV virus going around. A lot of people think these things will never happen to their kid. 'Oh my kid won't get caught behind the wheel drunk,' and so on. But at the end of every show I ever do I say, 'If you've been drinking or using dope, please make sure you get somebody around to drive you home, or leave your car and get a cab, 'cos I want to come back next year and do this again.' And that's the last message I leave the kids with, because some of these kids really go over the edge—at any concert—it's a party atmosphere."

(2001)

"Well, if you were going to have sex, you had to shove your willy somewhere. But, you know, been a long time since those days. And you'd always end up paying one way or another. I'd be lying in bed thinking, 'Have I got the fucking clap, or something else?' It would drive me insane by the end of the week."

(Observer, 2007)

"I met a girl—Thelma—and got married. I was very young and I shouldn't have done. It just all happened so quickly the success. I just thought I'd get married, get a house, have kids, that's what you do. It was just like somebody flicked a coin in the air and that was my life and it landed the right way up."

(Sunday Times, 2005)

"I'll be OK as long as there's me and my wife, and my kids and my group. But sometimes I start to wonder if my family's going to wait for me. I wonder if she'll get pissed off while I'm running around, recording and all. I don't know what I'd do without her."

(Rolling Stone, 1971)

"I got married way too young and I had children way too young."

(I Am Ozzy, 2009)

"I phoned my wife one time and I couldn't tell her where I was. I can only remember places like New York, San Francisco, and Los Angeles. It's like traveling the length of Britain daily. When you do get a break you can't get it together. You suddenly stop running and you don't know where you are or what to do with yourself."

(Disc, 1972)

"I spend more time in America, but it's only while my kids go to school. We suffer in our family with dyslexia and attention deficit disorder so they all—except Amy, who said bollocks to it—go to special schools. As soon as they're done, I'm out of here like a bat out of hell. The good thing about Los Angeles is everything's a third of the price to buy, the bad thing is everybody buys five times as much as they need. The weather's nice in LA, but you can't beat a good plate of fish and chips. My coat-of-arms loo is in England. I can't wait to get back home and show my ass to the coat of arms."

(Mojo, 2000)

"One time, I wanted to get a fucking black cathedral built in back of my house. She freaked and wouldn't allow it."

(Circus, 1980)

"If I loved Thelma, I certainly didn't treat her like I did. For years I acted like a married bachelor, sneaking around. I put that woman through hell. I should never have married her. She didn't deserve it, she wasn't a bad person and she wasn't a bad wife. But I was a fucking nightmare."

(I Am Ozzy, 2009)

"Fucking groupies. I'm telling you, the next one who pushes herself at me, I'm going to piss all over her. Me and Bill decided to do that. They're disgusting. Remember, Bill, that time in Atlanta, Georgia? This bitch called me on the telephone and said, 'I'm the best plater in the world (you know, blow job), can I come up to your room?' So I gave her Geezer's room number, and told her to come up, just for a laugh. Well, she went up to Geezer's room, and without a word took all her clothes off, and lay down on the bed with her legs apart, Billy, me, and Geezer looking on. 'Well, isn't somebody going to fuck me?' she says to us. We all just stood there looking at her, kind of horrified. She looked pitiful and disgusting. Finally, she got pissed off when no one went near her, got up and dressed. 'You English boys are disappointing.' A bunch of fags, she called us, and left the room. But the next time I'm not going to stand there. I'll fucking piss all over them. Wait till me mother reads that, she'll never speak to me again."

(Rolling Stone, 1971)

🤘

"(The Queen of England) said, 'I understand you're quite the wild one.' I just went, 'Heh, heh, heh'."

"There was this bird once who I thought I'd pulled. I thought she was a bit funny 'cos she didn't smoke or drink. When she got back to the hotel room she started on about being a redeemer and how I was polluted and how she was gonna save my soul...She learnt how to fly in less than a minute."

(Sounds, 1981)

"Sharon's never cooked a fucking dinner in her life—thank God for Domino's pizzas, I say. And with three teenage kids, it's hard to have sex. They say, 'We know what you're doing in there, you dirty pair of old bastards' or 'We can't go in there, dad's dry-humping mum again.' If I'd dared to say what they say to my dad, I'd be lying in the garden with a pitchfork stuck in my fucking chest."

(Mojo, 2000)

"I wanted to call my daughter (Aimee) Burt Reynolds, but my wife wouldn't have it."

(1982)

"Ever since Kelly was born she has what we call a 'wobbler.' It's kind of like a freak-out. Blaaaahhhhh! Waaaaa! Over nothing! She's had a wobbler every day since she's being living. So when you say, 'what causes...,' it's Kelly!"

"Jack, stop telling people you're Ozzy Osbourne's son to get into places, you're a fucking loser!"

"My son (Jack) is a miracle. Three years ago he was on this oxycodone, this hillbilly heroin—it's a time-release painkiller and if you do some weird shit to it, you get stoned. But he went away and got fixed and then he's on television climbing a mountain. I'm so proud of him as I am of all my children. They have lived through this tidal wave when we went into this Beatles-Elvis zone of popularity when we stopped fucking traffic in the street. It was unbelievable."

(Sunday Times, 2005)

"This love trip is so grossly distorted. One week you fall in love, the next week you fall out and start doing dope and blow your mind out. I don't believe there's anyone in this world who is 100 percent in love."

(1972)

"(Kelly)…you haven't been
playing doctors and nurses have you?"

"To be a parent, especially to rock 'n' roll kids,
I think being a parent is the most difficult job on
the face of the earth. You hate to say things that
will upset your kids, but then sometimes you have
to because you can't let them run around wild."

"I'm very computer dumb. My son goes,
'Dad, check this out.' He sits up there in his
room for fucking four days playing this thing
going, 'Shhh! Don't get me going!' I'm very slow
with the computers; I'm one of the old timers. But
it's the future, you know. My kids now—when I
was a kid, the big thing with my dad was learning
how to work the remote, and I learned that, so I
thought, 'I'll always know what's going on.' But
now my kids are talking in fucking computer
language—megabytes and gigabytes,
whatever the fuck that means."

(ign.com, 2009)

"Every time I mention the vagina doctor,
you get this little smirk on your face.
What have you been up to?"

—*Talking to Kelly*

"One day, my son and I were arguing
and he said, 'Do you mind if people laugh
with you, or at you?' And I said I didn't give a
shit, so long as they were laughing. But really,
I was thinking I wouldn't like to know for
a fact that they're laughing at me."

"I'm the guy kids love and parents hate.
The guy mothers love to hate. When you've
achieved that, you've achieved a goal."

CHAPTER 10

REALITY TV

he first years of the 21st century continued to be as hectic for Ozzy as the last years of the 20th. The Black Sabbath reunion continued, at least on stage, and Ozzfest grew bigger and bigger.

But what really nailed Ozzy and his family to the wall of public awareness was the fall 2001 debut of *The Osbournes*, an MTV sitcom/documentary in which five solid months of family life were laid open to public inspection.

The runaway hit of the fall season, *The Osbournes* became the most successful show in the network's history, earning Sharon an Emmy for her production duties, and prompting a flood of Osbourne-related ephemera onto the market. Neither was its success confined to its absurd novelty value alone.

Though the much-anticipated second season of *The Osbournes* was overshadowed by news that Sharon had cancer (she subsequently recovered), daughter Kelly would spin off a successful recording career, topping the UK charts with a duet with her dad, while Osbourne's own publicized bouts with ill health (including a serious fall while out biking) also proved incapable of stopping him.

Sharon, too, bounced back, becoming a judge on the television talent shows, *The X Factor* and *America's Got Talent;* penning a multi-million selling autobiography, *Extreme*, and hosting her own chat shows and securing advertising contracts. In 2009, she was ranked the 25th richest woman in Britain on the *Sunday Times'* annual Rich List; she and Ozzy together are ranked the 724th richest people in Britain, with an estimated joint wealth of £110 million (about $150 million in US dollars).

❝...as you'll know, the word 'fuck' sort of is used quite a lot in my house. Now, that's not to say, I think to say 'Fuck this' or 'Fuck you' a lot more, so it should be entered into the English language, because it has a lot more impact when you say, 'I fucking hate this thing.' ❞

(MTV.com, 2002)

❝I am a clown. You're asking me a serious question and I'm answering you in a civilized manner if you can make out what I'm saying. I only watched one show, it touched a bad nerve in me...all they were doing was waiting for me to trip up or tread in dog shit. People loved me as a likeable fool, as fucking Norman Wisdom, but I'm not like that all the time.❞

(Sunday Times, 2005)

"People thought (*The Osbournes)* was scripted but it wasn't. They'd sit there with five cameras pointing in all directions just for you to slip on a dog turd or something."

"I love you all. I love you more than life itself, but you're all fucking mad."

"What you see on the show is absolutely us."

"Oh, wonderful, we'll live here."

"I'm not picking up dog shit. I'm a rock star."

"It's as if I went to bed in one world and woke up in a completely different world. We went down to this market in Beverly Hills where you can just walk around artwork and statues and dolls and all this stuff and I got this really creepy feeling. I look around. People aren't looking, but I could feel eyes on me. I thought I was getting paranoid or something.**"**

"No we won't—no we won't break the law, Sharon.**"**

"I'm a very simple man. You've got to have, like, a computer nowadays to turn the TV on and off...and the nightmare continues.**"**

"Turn that thing off, it's driving me mad!**"**

Before he found fame on TV, Ozzy also appeared on the big screen in the 1986 rock-n-roll horror movie, *Trick or Treat*. Also in the movie are Tony Fields, center, and Gene Simmons of KISS. Ozzy plays a preacher who condemns heavy-metal music for being evil.

"I just wish everybody would back
off and leave my family alone, you know?**"**
(1989)

"I don't really like television. Sharon
keeps going on about including me in the
conversation and I go, 'Sharon, hang on a minute,
let's talk before WE do this television show. I
want to know what WE—meaning me, the other
part of we, as you being part of we and me being
the other part of we—I want to know what this
half of the we wants to do, what the fuck I'm
getting myself in for because I'm no fucking
weatherman. I've been working a long time on
the road and I want to take a vacation on a boat
I can do that. Then this fucking *X-Factor* comes
on the television and I'm a lonely guy on
Saturday nights you know.**"**
(Sunday Times, 2005)

"I like warming my butt by the fire.**"**

"I live in a 9 million dollar turd."

"The thing is, I feel that most of my life has
been worthless and useless, and I'm now at
the age where I'm beginning to feel that way."

(Rolling Stone, 2000)

"I really liked *Silence of the Lambs*,
and I must have watched *The Exorcist* eight
billion times. And my daughter, Amy, gets into it.
She loves horror films. It disturbs me. I know it
sounds kind of weird for me, Ozzy Osbourne, to
say that those movies make me so uncomfortable.
But I like to watch pleasant things."

(2001)

"(When Sharon was diagnosed with
colon cancer) I freaked out. She's the love
of my life, and she's also, like, the controller.
I couldn't sleep with her for nine months
because I was scared of waking up
and she'd died in the night."

"I just can't wake from these scary dreams."

"(Sharon) never knows when to say, 'Right, that's it, I'm going home, I'm fucking tired.' She's survived colon of the cancer, she's had chemotherapy and when she gets a bee in her bonnet, you can't fucking tell her to calm down. She's unstoppable."

(Classic Rock, 2004)

"What do you want me to do with my gun Sharon? Put it under my bed? I'll put it under my bed!"

"It's like when we had the reality show. I had no fucking idea what we'd done. Straight people would come up to me stunned. I remember being in Boston, this is a story I tell a lot, and I'm coming out of the hotel, and this woman comes up to me and says, 'Ozzy Osbourne! What are you doing here?' I said, 'I'm here to do a show.' 'What show?' 'A rock and roll show.' 'Oh,' she said, 'you do that as well?' She had no idea that I was a rock and roll singer; she thought I was just a TV guy."

(IGN.com, 2009)

"We're the Osbournes, and I love it."

"I suppose Americans get a kick out of watching a crazy Brit family like us make complete fools of ourselves every week."

"There was this thing that said: 'Ozzy Osbourne refuses to grow old.' But I've got no choice. I'm not 21 any more."

(Observer, 2007)

CHAPTER 11

HEALTHY LIVING THE OZZY WAY

here is nothing more insufferable than a reformed former addict. You know exactly the sort of person, as well: the woman at work who was once a human ashtray, but now walks around with a look of interminable suffering plastered over her martyr-racked face, while fanning her nostrils should she even suspect that somebody has a pack of cigarettes in their pocket. And that's before she starts to talk about how desperately *hard* it was to quit, and how much *support* she received from her family, and how infinitely *healthier* she feels now that she's clean… and you almost feel guilty for wondering whether she was this bad-tempered before she took the cure.

Rock musicians are even worse. Because they don't just talk about their chemical salvation, they write songs about it as well.

"I hate that rehab shit!" lashed Brett Anderson, vocalist with the mid-1990s British superstars London Suede. "That's one place where America gets really suckered, with those rehab rock bands. Let me explain what going into rehab means. It means you're cool because you used to do drugs, but now you're a good lad, and you're really Nineties, so you want to give them up. But it's a complete excuse, and anybody who says it or does it is a complete careerist. I don't think the public should go out and buy records by people whose record companies have told them to say they're going into rehab. You want to talk about fakes and falseness in the music business…this rehab rock thing is such a lot of dog shit."

Well, that's a little harsh, isn't it? What about those poor souls who, without the timely intervention of some caring friends and psychiatrists, might now be dead, or gibbering basket cases? What about those people for whom drink and drugs and all the other personal problems that we're now being told are addictions and illnesses (why do you never hear about obese sex addicts?) truly are a crippling burden, without which their life would be radically improved?

And what about Ozzy...the one man out of all of them who can actually make cleaning up sound *fun*?

> **"**My therapist said, 'You're like a man in front of two doorways. You open one and there's a guy standing behind it with a baseball bat who smacks you 'round the head. Every time you open that door he smacks you, then one day you walk through the other door and nobody's there and you're feeling weird that you didn't get a smack so you go back through the first door, because it's what you're used to.' **"**
>
> *(Independent, 1996)*

> **"**I fucking hate Christmas. I fucking hate it. Everything stops. When I used to drink, it was a good excuse to get fucked for two weeks. Now I just hate it.**"**
>
> *(Daily Express, 2010)*

"I never take dope or anything before I go on stage."
(1978)

"I have a non-specific tremor compounded by Parkinson syndrome from taking coke for so many years."
(Mojo)

"I still take medication, but not for fun."

"I think it's terrible that young kids at school are getting junked out. I did Hammersmith the other night, and they were carrying these kids out who were sniffing glue! It's getting ridiculous."
(Creem, 1986)

"I've got into this habit of rubbing my shoulder because there's this big piece of metal inside my body, I can feel it. But that accident didn't slow me down. They wanted to keep me in hospital because my heart actually stopped beating twice—and they had to drain the blood out of my lungs. I was drowning in my own blood. But I didn't know anything about that. I was in a coma."
(Classic Rock, 2004)

"I know this guy who was a bone bender—what do you call it?—a chiropractor! He's also got a sort of clinic where he does hydro. Hydro! You know, they sort of suck off all the shit out of your body, clean your whole system out. He says red meat is fucking disgusting shit. It stays in there forever."

(Spin, 1986)

"I was drinking like a fish for two years. It was just getting worse and worse, off one thing and on to another. Finally I nearly ended up an alcoholic. We'd come offstage, for instance, and I'd just go straight to the bar. Perhaps I'd meet one of the band there, but I wouldn't drink for the sake of having a good time. I'd just drink to get out of the way. And that's when you've got to say to yourself, 'Hey man, there's something wrong.' You're just going through the day, just to get on the stage for an hour to do your gig, just to go home, get stoned, and go to bed. The next day's the same. There was no excitement. I would have been dead in two or three years if I'd carried on. I know I would. And I don't think anything's worth giving your life up for."

(NME, 1977)

"I've made some bad decisions, like when I decided to come back paralytic and attack my wife. That wasn't a very good decision, although I've no knowledge of doing it. Still, whatever made me get here today worked for me.**"**

(Daily Express, 2010)

"I thought to myself, 'Do I really enjoy getting drunk? Do I really enjoy coke?' And the answer was no, I'd rather have a fucking cup of tea.**"**

(Daily Express, 2010)

"The first thing I gave up was cigarettes. I'd been smoking any fucking thing. Don't ask me how I did that but I don't miss them. Once in every blue moon, I think, 'Ooh, a cigarette!' But then I think it through and, by 12 pm, I'd be smoking cigarette cartons again. I can't have one of any fucking thing.**"**

(Daily Express, 2010)

"The doctor can fuck himself.**"**

"I don't blame rock 'n' roll for my addiction—
it's my fault, and I've got to fight it. But it'd be
good if we could all do just one gig, like the Band
Aid thing, and build a proper clinic for them, like
the Betty Ford Center. That place really opened
my eyes. I was so embarrassed to go and get help.
I said, 'Me? Ozzy International blah-blah? I've got
to tell them I'm sick?' But I couldn't fight it any
more. I did my 15 rounds and I couldn't go out for
a 16th. It was killing me, and I didn't want to die."

(Creem, 1986)

"If I don't like being straight,
it's so very easy to become unstraight."

(Classic Rock, 2004)

"How many other jobs do you know where they go:
'It's going to be a great day today, he's out of his
fucking mind!' I was the guy parents loved to hate.
They used to say: 'Lock up your daughters, dog,
bat, Ozzy Osbourne is coming to town.' And now?
Now I don't drink any more, I don't do drugs any
more, I don't smoke cigarettes any more. I'm just
this boring middle-aged rock star."

(Observer, 2007)

❝It got to the point where I really hated myself. I saw that if I didn't do something about it, I was probably going to end up killing myself—or worse, I'd wind up murdering someone else…❞

(Hit Parader, 1985)

❝I think we all have regrets, but you can't say, 'Yeah, I should have fucking done that.' You know the definition of insanity is doing the same thing twice but expecting a different result. I'm proud of what I've achieved in my life. I'm a very, very lucky man. You couldn't have written my life story if you'd been the best writer in the world.❞

(Sunday Times, 2005)

❝I've done a lot of shit and bad stuff to my body, so why ruin the years I've got left on this planet? I want to try to do some good stuff. I mean, I lit the fucking candle at both ends. People have died doing half as much as me. But at the end of the day I wasn't really having fun with it. It didn't work for me. It was fucking awful.❞

(MusicToob, 2009)

"Oh yeah: I've had my double chin removed, and the fat Hoovered out from around my jaw line. But I've never had Botox. My philosophy is that if something makes you unhappy every time you look in the mirror, just do something about it. But it's like tattoos. (He looks fondly down at his own heavily decorated arm.) Once you have one, you have two…look at Michael Jackson: by the end, his sister La Toya looked more like him than he did."

(Telegraph, 2009)

✝

"When I went to my dentist the other day somebody told me they'd been on a holiday to the Caribbean. They went to this bar and this guy goes, 'Do you know who that guy is over there?' And they say no and it's Keith Richards, drunk. Who am I to say it's wrong? He enjoys it, it's his life. If I could enjoy it, then I'd drink."

(MusicToob, 2009)

"The human body's an incredible thing, because the amount of poison I put through my fucking self, I should be dead a thousand times."

(Uncut, 1997)

"I've seen literally thousands of doctors over my lifetime, and spent well over £1 million ($1.5 million Cdn) on them, to the point where I sometimes think I know more about being a doctor than doctors do."

—*Announcing he'll be writing a heath advice column for the Sunday Times magazine titled The Wisdom of Oz, and he'll sign it as "Dr. Ozzy," (June 2010)*

"Without (Sharon) behind me, I'd have been dead in the fucking water years ago. I'm a living miracle— I'm sitting here talking to you at two o clock in the afternoon stone cold sober, and breathing, you know. Better guys have died before me."

(Classic Rock, 2004)

"Viagra's a great sleeping drug. I take Viagra, and Sharon goes right to sleep."

"I try to live in the moment. I could be happy now but, ten minutes on, I'll be unhappy. We all have regrets but you get to a crossroads and you go left, right, or straight on. Whatever decision you make, you've got to live with it."

(Daily Express, 2010)

“At one time I was a happy guy when I
had a few drinks or dope or whatever, and then
I just got miserable and depressed. So I thought,
‘What the fuck am I doing this for?’ My biggest
addiction these days is exercise. I run every day.
I’ll probably be next to Jimmy Savile next
year running the fucking marathon!”

(Mojo, 2000)

“I only take pills now for clinical reasons, not to
get stoned any more. All the stuff I did left me
with some neurological problems—I’m a manic
depressive, a nutter. Sharon says she’ll second that.”

(Mojo, 2000)

“By far the most addictive thing I’ve ever put in my
body is tobacco. By the end, I was chewing the gum,
smoking the fake cigarettes, wearing the patches
and smoking 20 a day. I tried cigars, but within a
week I was smoking 30 Cohibas a day, and inhaling.
Now I don’t do anything any more. I got bored of
always being fucked up on something or other.”

(Telegraph, 2009)

“I’m sick and tired of being sick and tired.”

66 When I first got involved with rock 'n' roll, I thought the equipment was a bag of drugs, a crazy attitude, and a wild party at the end of the gig. That's honestly what I believed rock 'n' roll was. And it's not. 99

(Creem, 1986)

66 I know a lot of people who've taken cocaine, including myself, a lot of people who've smoked dope, including myself, a lot of people who've taken a lot of things—but I've never really taken heroin, only once or twice. Everybody that I know that's taken heroin is either a mental case or dead. Or they end up zombies. Even if you stop taking it, you never return to the person you were before; you end up screwed up for the rest of your life. 99

(Creem, 1986)

66 Somebody said to me this morning, 'To what do you attribute your longevity?' I don't know. I mean, I couldn't have planned my life out better. By all accounts I should be dead! The abuse I put my body through: the drugs, the alcohol, the lifestyle I've lived the last 30 years! Now, some rare fly will fly over me, crap on my shoulder, and I'll drop dead, you know? My life story is a real-life story. 99

(Launch.com, 1998)

"I have this thing called acid reflux. Causes all kinds of problems with my voice. As I get older, there are more and more delights that I'm having to leave by the wayside. I can't eat chocolate, I can't eat this, I can't eat that. You think the older you get, you'd be able to eat what the fuck you like because you're going to die soon anyway."

(Classic Rock, 2004)

"I've been taking Prozac for the last four years, because I had a chemical imbalance. I went ultra-paranoid. It did some lasting damage, the abuse, so now I'm a health freak. I work out every day, I eat as little animal fat as possible. We eat a bit of turkey. It's a little known fact that the turkey is a relative of the vulture, y'know? And some of the McCartney stuff. Vegetarian stuff. Or there's a place in Beaconsfield where you can get brown rice out of a can."

(Uncut, 1997)

"All I have to say is this: sobriety fucking sucks!"

CHAPTER 12

THE WORLD IN GENERAL

A miscellany of motley murmurings, as the Ozz-meister leads us through all the bits that wouldn't fit elsewhere. Gun control, personal hygiene, cutting edge technology, insect urine, death, and more—the Master of Reality offers us a sobering glimpse into the state of planet Earth, as seen through a mind that may not be quite as crazy as you think.

❝It's gettin' crazy. It's like watching the rise and fall of the Roman Empire. Being an outsider... I spend a lot of time in America, but I am a foreign person... and I really do love this country, but watching the different political changes and fashions, I see it going from happy faces to anger. I don't know why they're angry. Whether they're getting high on some weird shit or what, I don't know. It's kind of very radical.❞

(Spin, 1986)

MILLION SELLING OZZY

BLACK SABBATH (1970) — 1 MILLION SOLD (PLATINUM)
PARANOID (1971) — 4 MILLION SOLD (QUADRUPLE PLATINUM)
MASTER OF REALITY (1971) — 2 MILLION SOLD (DOUBLE PLATINUM)
VOLUME FOUR (1972) — 1 MILLION SOLD (PLATINUM)
SABBATH BLOODY SABBATH (1974) — 1 MILLION SOLD (PLATINUM)
SABOTAGE (1975) — 1 MILLION SOLD (PLATINUM)
WE SOLD OUR SOUL FOR ROCK 'N' ROLL (COMPILATION, 1976) — 2 MILLION SOLD
(DOUBLE PLATINUM)
THE BLIZZARD OF OZ (1981) — 4 MILLION SOLD (QUADRUPLE PLATINUM)
DIARY OF A MADMAN (1981) — 3 MILLION SOLD (TRIPLE PLATINUM)
SPEAK OF THE DEVIL (LIVE, 1982) — 1 MILLION SOLD (PLATINUM)
BARK AT THE MOON (1983) — 3 MILLION SOLD (TRIPLE PLATINUM)
THE ULTIMATE SIN (1986) — 2 MILLION SOLD (DOUBLE PLATINUM)
TRIBUTE (LIVE, 1987) — 2 MILLION SOLD (DOUBLE PLATINUM)
NO REST FOR THE WICKED (1988) — 2 MILLION SOLD (DOUBLE PLATINUM)
NO MORE TEARS (1991) — 4 MILLION SOLD (QUADRUPLE PLATINUM)
LIVE AND LOUD (LIVE, 1993) — 1 MILLION SOLD (PLATINUM)
OZZMOSIS (1995) — 2 MILLION SOLD (DOUBLE PLATINUM)
THE OZZMAN COMETH (COMPILATION, 1997) — 2 MILLION SOLD (DOUBLE PLATINUM)
REUNION (LIVE, 1998) — 1 MILLION SOLD (PLATINUM)
DOWN TO EARTH (2001) — 1 MILLION SOLD (PLATINUM)
LIVE AT BUDOKAN (LIVE, 2002) — 1 MILLION SOLD (PLATINUM)

"What is the world coming to?"

**"LA's not a good place to grow old. It's a
Paris Hilton-getting-fucked-up-the-ass kind
of town... a town full of ambulance chasers."**

"In my life, I went from radio to stereo, stereo to eight track cassettes where if you wanted to put the record in, you had to put this big thing in the fucking thing. Now, one thing I have is the iPod, which is fucking unbelievable. Sixty thousand songs! I don't know sixty fucking thousand songs! It's unbelievable! I don't understand it! I can't understand it."

(ign.com, 2009)

✝

"I don't know when videocassettes went out, you know, the VHS. I got every film I ever wanted on VHS. Now, I've got fucking shitloads of them and I can't even watch the film. It's unbelievable! Someone said to me that science fiction today is tomorrow's science fact. The next thing you're going to have is robots."

(ign.com, 2009)

"In America, there seems to be an awards show for everything. It used to be just the Grammys, the Oscars, and the Emmys over there, and now there's thousands of fucking awards shows. It's becoming a big showcase for people's egos. To be perfectly honest with you, I don't feel comfortable in those situations."

(Classic Rock, 2004)

"I love the smell of armpits
in the morning. It's like victory."

"In California you can't smoke a cigarette
in your own house but you can buy a gun
—that's one thing I don't understand."

(Independent, 2009)

"The idea of a band nowadays is five
pretty boys, one with a tattoo, one with a shaved
head, and on and on. What the fuck is that?
I mean, I like Britney Spears, I think she's
pretty, but I'm not from the Mickey Mouse Club.
I'm from the Godzilla Club!"

(Guitar World, 2000)

"In the States, violence is the fashion.
This month's fashion is hitting people
over the heads with bottles. Next month's
might be wearing pink socks."

(Melody Maker, 1975)

"This pea soup tastes like gnat's piss."

(Rolling Stone, 1971)

❝I sometimes get great ideas in the weirdest places and there's nothing you can do about it.❞

(Disc, 1972)

❝I like America, but I wouldn't live there because (a) there's a lot of guns about and a lot of people who would use them and (b) I don't want to be in the firing line. I'm frightened of the violence. I don't want to go there. Everybody else has gone to America. I don't want to be at the end of the queue. I want to start somewhere else off. How about China? That sounds good to me. Or Russia. What a trip that would be!❞

(Melody Maker, 1975)

❝I want to be American. America is the coolest place on the face of the Earth. You've got freedom of speech. You've got McDonald's.❞

❝I hate these fucking stretch bastards junk pimp mobiles!❞

"I think the business is fucked. There are too many people sitting on their assholes and doing nothing for vast amounts of money. There's so much talent out there who're so frightened to get involved, because they think they're going to end up floating down the River Thames in a pair of concrete Wellingtons. The business is like a rosy red apple at the front, with a big crab at the back."

(NME, 1977)

"We all have a little bit of a skeleton in our cupboard that we think, fuck, I don't want to talk about that again. But it don't really bother me, if I can help it. It's like saying, 'I wish I hadn't bought a red car.' You bought it, so drive it."

(Spin, 1986)

"Whoever invented those mobile phones with cameras needs fucking shooting."

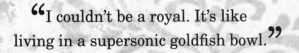

"I couldn't be a royal. It's like living in a supersonic goldfish bowl."

Ozzy arrives at the Elton John AIDS Foundation's sixth annual benefit, "An Enduring Vision," at The Waldorf-Astoria Hotel in 2007.

"This has all been such an amazing journey for me. I can vividly remember sitting on the step of my house in Aston, just tripping about what it would be like to be a Beatle. And then, here I am at 58, and I'm at (Elton John)'s party."

Chapter 13

In the End

❝I'd rather look good in my coffin than bad in my coffin. Fucking go for it. Can you imagine me at the age of 65 or fucking 70, singing, 'I once was fucking vaudeville, remember him?' That's not my fucking style, man. Burn out with a flash. I don't give a flying fuck about myself any more.❞

(1982)

❝I was in a cab the other day and the bloke says, 'Are you in a group?' I said yeah and he said who, and I said Ozzy Osbourne. And he said, 'I know him! He's the one who bites the heads off animals!' And I think...what a horrible thing to leave behind. Ozzy Osbourne, the man who used to bite the heads off animals! It's not a very good legacy, is it?❞

(NME, 1986)

> 66 I'd like to buy a little pub somewhere and remember what I've done. Being behind a bar's a lot like entertaining. You're keeping people happy. 99
>
> *(1978)*

> 66 I'm about caring, I'm about people, and I'm about entertaining people. I'm a family man. A husband. A father. I've been a lot of other things over the years, which we don't really want to talk about. 99
>
> *(Launch.com, 10/30/1998)*

> 66 I'm always working on trying to better myself, you know? I think that that is an ongoing thing with me. I think I'll do that for the rest of my life. I'm always thinking of what I can do today to better my life. 99
>
> *(Launch.com, 10/30/1998)*

> 66 I feel like I'm invisible. 99

> 66 I sold my soul for this game. 99
>
> *(1978)*

"I'll only retire in the day I should be dead and they have me buried, and some idiot spell over my casket some stupid gospel stuff."

"Heroin is awful. Look what happened to poor old Phil Lynott. So many rock stars have died now, look at them! I'm not saying I'm any better than Phil Lynott or Keith Moon—I'm luckier, that's all."

(Creem, 1986)

"How the fuck do you feed a tree? What... you put a ham sandwich on the tree?"

"I'll die before I'm 40."

(Rolling Stone, 1971)

"What's left to wish for? A number one album would be good. And to have a movie made of the book, maybe with Johnny Depp playing me. I'd like that."

(2010)

❝I said, 'Jack, don't just do things that make me look like a fucking saint. I'm not a saint.' Because, you know, you see some guy on the biography channel or something, and they'll say how wonderful he is. Well, even Jesus Christ wasn't always wonderful. Isn't there one time when he goes, 'Fuck, I don't feel like giving a speech on this mountain.'?❞

—On his son filming a documentary of sorts on his famous father (Goldmine, 2010)

❝This will end in tears.❞

❝You bastards.❞

(Sabbath Bloody Sabbath, 1973)

✝

❝They say life sucks and then you die. That's pretty much it.❞

❝It's good fun and it's had great rewards. It's been such an eye opener for me. Everything that I have ever wanted to have has come from rock and roll. I've had happiness, I've had sadness. I've had everything. I've experienced life, death, birth, marriage, divorce, and it's been a whole bunch of fun. I wouldn't have it any different. I'd do it all again tomorrow.❞

FROM ONE ROCK LEGEND TO ANOTHER

Some 30 years after his death, John Lennon's genius as a musician, artist, songwriter, singer, social activist and member of the human race continues to be celebrated and cherished at an iconic level.

In this superb book from noted music journalist John M. Borack, the life, music, influence and attitude of this legendary lad from Liverpool is captured in fascinating stories, personal reflections from fans and celebrities, and hundreds of photographs of the Beatles, Lennon and Ono, and the people and places that made up their world. In addition you'll see photographs of various Beatles and Lennon memorabilia, along with dozens of quotes from Lennon himself.

John Lennon: Life is What Happens
Music, Memories & Memorabilia
Softcover • 10" x 10" • 256 p
500 color and b&w photos
Item# Z7968 • $26.99

"I'd like to say 'thank you'
on behalf of the group and
ourselves and I hope we
passed the audition."

~ John Lennon, Jan. 30, 1969